The Distance Learner

Written by
Sharon Roberts and David Muir

Designed by
Jane Gibbs

Developed from the book
Extension Study Skills
by Malcolm Potter

Published by **St John's Extension Studies**
Bramcote, Nottingham NG9 3RL

© St John's Nottingham 1994, 1995, 1996, 1997, 2001, 2006

ISBN 1-900920-00-X

Many of the photographs used are from www.morguefile.co.uk

Printed in Great Britain by AT Print Services Ltd., Thurnscoe, Rotherham S63 0UB

Other resources available from St John's are listed on the end pages of this workbook, or visit www.stjohns-nottm.ac.uk for a comprehensive and up-to-date list. Bulk copies of this book are available at significantly reduced prices, to help resource other Christian learning programmes. Bookshops can obtain the usual trade discounts, on this and other workbooks in the Faith for Life series.

Study skills weekends are currently held annually at St John's Nottingham. A separate leaflet and booking form is available.

For all the above, please phone 0115 925 1117

Contents

Who this book is for

More and more Christians are deciding that they want to study the Christian faith for themselves. They are not content any more with titbits from the pulpit. There are a number of distance learning programmes now available. This book is mostly designed to help Christians get the best out of them.

It seeks to combine good advice from 'how to study' books with insights from adult education. The evidence is that books on how to study fail to help those who most need it. They tend to help those who already *know* they can study. So we address attitude and lifestyle as well as trying to be practical about the actual study process.

We have tried to keep particularly in mind those whose previous experience of education (especially school) has been a negative one. For the others, we apologise for returning to this point again and again. But we still live with the legacy of a past system where only 5% achieved A levels and only 20% achieved O levels. The other 80% were often given the impression that

they had failed. They have carried this feeling with them into adulthood. It is our conviction that this is the single greatest barrier to their succeeding in higher education. Sometimes it is the only barrier.

We have also tried to integrate into this a Christian perspective on studying our faith. It has been known for people to lose their faith in the labyrinths of university theology. We are concerned that this should not happen. In our experience the study of theology strengthens faith and commitment, making it more mature and sturdy. This is the primary concern of chapter 7, but we hope it pervades the whole book.

Although this workbook is written for those in distance learning, there is much here to help the new student of Christian theology in residential colleges and other forms of part-time theological study. They face many of the same issues. Here is a useful preparation and a handy reference guide in the early days of their studies.

How to use this book

This is a workbook - designed for you to interact with it and think through the issues raised. It is meant to be *used*, not just *read*. If you keep it pristine, you will limit the amount you learn. We hope you will write and scribble notes in it, mark some bits and write rude comments against others.

We have put the chapters in what seems like a logical order. But you might find it easier to work through them in a different order. You might even want to remove the binding, punch holes and file them uyour own way.

People learn study skills as they actually *do* the study they want to do. You can't learn all about studying by reading this book beforehand. So use this workbook alongside your study programme. If

you take the St John's New Testament Introduction course unit, you will find the relevant parts of this workbook keyed into those study materials at appropriate places.

This book also forms the basis for Study Skills Weekends at St Johns Nottingham, sponsored by the Open Theological College. This is an opportunity to work through the principles outlined in this book in conversation with tutors and other students like yourself. Details can be obtained from St John's Extension Studies.

More than anything else, we hope and pray that your study will deepen your relationship with God and broaden your contribution to the life and work of the church. Studying is a discipleship issue.

Can adults learn?

This chapter will help you to think about what studying as an adult is like, the joys as well as the struggles. It will focus on the learning you have already done during your life and how this might help you with the more organised learning you are about to embark on.

Contents

As soon as we think of 'studying', our minds often turn to our school days. After all, school is where we all came into contact with the practice of studying. Perhaps even now you can summon up the noises of the classrooms, the squeak of chalk on the board and the smell of school dinners...

Perhaps your school or college days were the best days of your life and there are plenty of happy memories. If that is the case then returning to study may well be something you are looking forward to and something you approach with a certain amount of confidence.

But for many people school days were not a happy experience and hold memories of frustration and failure. If this is true for you, then you may be returning to studying with a considerable amount of anxiety. What if the same thing happens all over again?

Most adults tend to underestimate their ability to learn by giving far too much emphasis to their school experience. Studying as an adult is very different from studying at school.

Have you left school?

Who's in charge?

Just for a moment think back to the way things were at school... Who decided what you were going to study? Who decided how, when and where you were going to learn? Did you have any choice in whether you were going to learn at all or was it simply assumed that you were going to?

It was probably the teacher who was in charge. S/he was responsible for what you learnt and how you learnt it.

You are a free agent – no one is making you study. No one is going to tell you what you must learn. As an adult learner you choose what you are going to study and when you are going to study. You are in charge. You decide your priorities. You decide your targets and how you are going to achieve them.

Being in charge may seem quite frightening but it doesn't need to be. As we shall see, there are ways in which you can make learning work for you in a way that will help you to achieve the goals you have set.

Learning as a child and learning as an adult are different. The question is: who is in control? And the answer is that – now – you are!

Wealth not poverty

In the past many schoolteachers saw their pupils as empty vessels which needed filling up. Even if that is partially true of children, it certainly isn't true of adults. All adults come to new learning with a wealth of experience of life. This is a great advantage. Experience means that you already have a framework of knowledge to fit new ideas into.

Think for a moment about someone who is learning to drive. Even before they get their hands on the wheel most people will be aware of which side of the road to drive on, have seen some road signs, be aware of the dangers of speed and so on.

When we are studying our faith, our experience and knowledge of God is a valuable resource. Sometimes our experience of life will force us to mistrust easy or pat answers and send us deeper into the problem we are studying – with more satisfying results. Never underestimate the wealth of experience which you as an adult bring to your new learning experience.

Tutors not teachers

Perhaps you remember your first day at school:

- The teacher seemed to tower above you.
- The teacher seemed to have the most effective pair of lungs you had ever heard.
- The teacher never seemed to lose any opportunity of making sure you realised that you were only a child, someone who should only speak when spoken to.

Well, the good news is that you are now an adult! The relationship you should expect to have with your tutor is an adult-to-adult relationship. When you start a course of learning you don't become a child again. You are your tutor's equal in every way except for the expertise they have in a particular subject area. It is up to both of you to make sure it stays a partnership of equals.

THINK BACK

What years were you at school?

From   to

What kind of world was it then? Think of some things that happened in the world during those years. How much has changed? How much have you changed?

Success not failure

Perhaps school holds memories of failure for you. Failing the 11+, or an important exam. Perhaps it meant never being in the top group for anything. And perhaps exams always seemed to test what you didn't know rather than what you did.

There is no reason why a learning course for adults should be about failing all over again. A great deal of thought has gone into the workbooks you will be using, and they are written just for adults. Often there will be opportunities for you to test yourself. Adult learning packages are designed to help you to succeed. And the rest of this book will give you hints at how to achieve that successful learning more easily.

Adults do learn!

You didn't stop learning the minute you left school. In fact, for most people the learning process speeds up as we enter the 'real world'.

Learning is something adults do all the time – often without even trying. We 'learn' when we read the newspaper and when we watch the TV. We 'learn' about new people when we meet them. We are always learning.

The truth of the matter is that we never stop learning. The trouble is that we rarely stop to think about all that we learn.

So stop now and think for a moment about something that you have learnt to do successfully in the last year. In the home – how to wire a plug, programme the new video, or cook a new recipe. It might be part of a hobby – a set of rules for a game or a new physical skill of some kind. Or it might be something at work – perhaps you have had to take on a new job, or learnt to work with a different set of people. Remember to choose something you learnt successfully, no matter how insignificant it may seem.

One thing that I have learnt successfully in the last year is.............

Now think about that learning experience......

Why did you learn it?

How did you go about learning it?

Who or what helped you learn?

What did you find difficult about this learning?

What happened when it was difficult?

How did you feel when the learning was finished?

Why was this particular piece of learning so successful? I suspect there were two main reasons.

Ready to learn

Have you ever wished you had paid more attention to the things you were taught at school? At the time, the things children are taught in school can seem irrelevant and boring, especially when there are more immediate and interesting things to think about! It is only when we leave school that we realise that those things were important.

At different points in our lives we become ready to learn different skills and information. To a young man of 22, rocking a baby to sleep or playing with a 9-year old may be things he 'can't really do'. The same man just a few years later with his own young children has a new reason to want to learn those things – he learns them fast, and (often!) enjoys it enormously. He is ready to learn – and so he does learn.

The very fact that you have taken the time and energy to write away for details of a course of theological study, apply for it and pay for it, suggests that you are 'ready to learn' theology. This means that the learning you do is likely to be successful.

Being selective

When he was nine, my son loved knowledge. He soaked up information. Like a sponge. Everything interested him. Apparently trivial and useless information was stored and remembered, kept in mind on a par with information that might save his life.

It was all right for him then. His mental filing system was not well developed and there was plenty of room in it! You and I are not like that. Our filing system is already quite extensive and there's not so much room left!

So we focus our learning. We become selective. We choose carefully what to learn, then we are choosy about what we pay attention to within that learning.

As adults we learn best when we are studying things we are convinced we need to know.

That is good for us. It helps us learn. In fact we need to function like this to learn effectively. If we feel obliged to learn everything that is put before us, without seeing its relevance to what we already know (where to put it in the filing system), then we are courting failure.

You need to learn like an adult, not like a child – because you are an adult!

...and the rest

Other valuable skills in learning successfully as an adult can be:

- Planning time helpfully
- Following an instruction manual
- Not being afraid to ask for help
- Persevering even when things get difficult

Three steps to learning

Learning has been described in many different ways. A helpful way of looking at it is to see that it has three main parts....

Taking in new ideas

Not simply about hearing new ideas or learning them off by heart. Taking in a new idea is about making sense of what is being said. It is about understanding.

Thinking through the ideas

Trying to fit the new idea into the rest of your knowledge on a subject. It often involves asking painful questions about whether you might have to rethink your previous ideas.

Working with the new ideas

Done in many different ways: maybe through a piece of writing for an assignment; maybe in a group as you discuss what you have read and heard; maybe through a change in how you act.

Practice makes perfect?

Have you ever listened to an accomplished pianist? If you were to ask the pianist about how they achieved such a standard, they would probably emphasise the need for practice. They would probably also go on to talk about the benefits of practising scales every day before going on to more demanding compositions.

There are parallells here with studying and learning skills. Developing your learning skills is something you can never do enough of. Even the most experienced students sometimes need to stop and think about the way they do things. Just as the pianist practises scales, the experienced 'studier' needs to practise the basic skills of adult learning. Whatever stage you have reached, there is always benefit from going back to the basics, examining your technique, and finding ways to improve. You will often find that the advice you need is not necessarily different from the advice given to a beginner. The basic skills remain the same but you need to understand and review them at a deeper level.

So, even if you are an experienced student, the advice in this book is for you. Use it to help you review the way you work at the moment. You may also find ideas that are relevant to other areas of your life and work as well as to this new course of study.

If you are new to study, don't worry! Even the experts have to keep practising, so you are not so far behind after all!

The skills you have

We have already seen that as adults we are learning all the time and learning with a great deal of success. Remember that learning doesn't just take place in school or a college or even in a work situation. It is part of our lives.

But some things are important for successful learning. Imagine a plumber turning up to fix a leaking pipe without any tools. You wouldn't be impressed, and without the tools it is doubtful if a successful job could be done. In the same way, there are certain skills and attitudes (we could call them 'tools') which we need in order to study. If we don't have them we will struggle with the more demanding learning tasks.

Have a go at filling in this questionnaire. All the descriptions are helpful skills and attitudes for an adult seeking to learn. Again, you may well find that you already have a number of really important skills and attitudes necessary for undertaking a course of study.

	Usually	Sometimes	Never
I know what I want to achieve			
I can set myself a target			
I can stick to a target			
I can ask others for help			
I can listen to other people's opinions			
I can take new ideas on board			
I can cope with constructive criticism			
I can concentrate on what interests me			
I don't give up easily			
I can work on my own			
I like to be independent			
I can gather information from magazines/TV/radio			
I am realistic about my achievements			
I can treat myself to a "reward" when I have achieved something			

How did you get on? I hope you found that you could tick the 'Sometimes' and 'Usually' boxes quite often. Did you notice that a lot of the descriptions referred to the sort of person you are and the attitudes you have? There are personal characteristics and attitudes which help you in the learning process. How you learn is linked to who you are. As an adult, the personal maturity and flexibility you bring to your studies will help a great deal.

Don't worry if you had to tick the 'never' box sometimes. The rest of this book will help you to think about and develop some of the learning skills you don't have already. It will also help you to develop those skills you do have. Studying will change you, whoever you are, and whatever your personality type! If you complete this questionnaire again at the end of your course of study you will find that the number of 'Usually's will be greater than at the moment. Try it and see!

Much of the material on these pages is based on Derek Rowntree's Teach Yourself with Open Learning *(Kogan Page, 1993)*

The steep slope of change

The educationalist R S Peters once wrote: 'to be educated is not to have arrived: it is to travel with a different view'. Often we are not prepared for this. The need for change can be hard to accept. We want to be the same people with more knowledge.

When you study theology you are studying something that impinges closely on your own faith. The content of the courses may well be quite different from anything you have ever come across before. You will be faced with new ideas and problems. This new knowledge may demand that we change our previous outlook on the world and even some of our ideas about God. This sort of change can be exciting but it can also be painful.

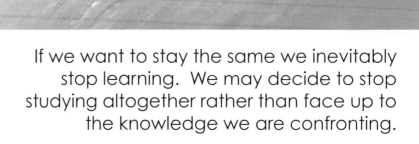

If we want to stay the same we inevitably stop learning. We may decide to stop studying altogether rather than face up to the knowledge we are confronting.

The impetus to learn

The more we learn, the more we realise how much there is still to learn. Knowledge can seem like a mountain that is impossible to scale. We are aware that our minds are not as nimble as they used to be. What is going to propel us up that steep slope?

Often we read about something in the papers or hear about something on TV and soon begin to think that we ought to know more about it. Christians are particularly susceptible to this frame of mind. How often have you heard Christians say 'Oh I really ought to read my Bible more often' or 'I really ought to know more about the background to the Bible'.

The weakness of ought

The 'I really ought' frame of mind is not a helpful starting place to embark on learning. 'I really ought' usually stems from a vague feeling of guilt. Do you remember as a child being told that you really ought to write a thank you letter to great aunt Nellie? Deep down, you knew you should too, but remember the arguments you had over doing it, the frustration of sitting down to write a letter when there were so many more interesting things you could have been doing? Guilt doesn't usually prove to be a strong motivating factor for anyone. Most of us don't like feeling guilty and will sooner or later give up and go and do something we enjoy more. Deciding to study because you feel guilty about how little you know will be like trying to push something much bigger than you are.

The strength of why

A better way is to ask a few big questions about what you want to achieve, and why. Spend some time thinking about the questions below. Use the boxes to keep a record of your answers. Later on in your studies, when it feels like a struggle, it will be good to remind yourself of these reasons.

Why have you enrolled on this course?

What do you really want to learn or get out of the course ?

Is there a specific thing you would like to be able to do as a result of completing the course?

Case studies

How much impetus to learn does each of these people have? In what ways are any of them like you?

Pam is a mother of three children who are all now at school. She has been promising herself time to learn more about her faith for years; sermons and Bible-study groups have left her thirsting for more. It took nine months for her to complete the course on the New Testament, and she found it fairly difficult, having done no study since school-days, where she scraped through a couple of GCSEs. Her husband is glad she is doing the course, though he'd really like her to get a part-time job so that they can think about changing the car next year.

Geoff's children are married now. His job is very demanding and he is now looking for early retirement. The church is wanting to develop a team of lay assistants and Geoff has been invited to be involved, and he feels a strong sense of calling. It was decided that all members of the team should undertake some theological study. Six candidates have made a start, but Geoff is struggling to keep up. He finds the material easy enough, if not 'beneath him' and he thinks his tutor is 'a bit wet behind the ears', so if he has a bad day he doesn't feel inclined to study in the evening.

Jane has been an office supervisor for ten years, though she has felt a strong call to full-time Christian work for some time. She would like to do a college course but her mother is a chronic invalid. Her minister is very caring but feels very much that Jane's place is with her mother. He refuses to discuss her sense of vocation at present. A friend has recommended doing a distance learning course and Jane is enjoying it immensely.

Studying to please others?

You may be studying theology by distance learning because it is a requirement for some particular ministerial training you are doing. If this is the case your motivating factors will be affected and you may not have the breadth of choice that other students have. You may well find that you are required to study certain topics which may not immediately interest you.

If this is the case, try to *find* an interest in the material at some level. Once you start, the course writer may draw you into the subject. On other occasions you might have to raise questions for yourself. Why is it that this subject is a requirement of the course? Why do other people find this interesting?

Try to pose a question that will make the subject more interesting for *you*.

Prayer back-up

If you find things are becoming difficult, perhaps you will need to ask 'Am I facing up honestly to what I am learning, or am I trying to run back to the security I had before?' If you decide that you are retreating to previous certainties, talk to your minister or contact your tutor. Working through your uncertainties to a place of greater security will in the end lead to a stronger faith. There are particular joys and struggles in studying your faith and more will be said about these in chapter 7.

> *I have heard of your faith in the Lord Jesus and your love toward all the saints, and for this reason I do not cease to give thanks for you as I remember you in my prayers. I pray that the God of our Lord Jesus Christ, the Father of glory , may give you the spirit of wisdom and revelation as you come to know him, so that, with the eyes of your heart enlightened, you may know what are the riches of his glorious inheritance among the saints, and what is the immeasurable greatness of his power for us who believe, according to the working of his great power.*
> *(Ephesians 1: 15-19)*

At the very beginning of your theological studies it might be good to find someone who can pray for you as you study. Look at the way St Paul prayed that the Ephesian Christians would grow in their knowledge of God.

The person you choose doesn't have to be able to pray like St. Paul. All they have to do is to promise to pray that God will help you and give you his spirit of wisdom as you study.

You might like to write in the names of those who are praying for you and who will pray with you when you ask them. When things are hard it is good to know that there are people prayerfully supporting you.....

Who is praying for me?

Coping with freedom

Before going on, spend some time looking back over this chapter. Then use the following questions for personal reflection. You might want to turn some of these thoughts into prayer....

As an adult studying on a distance learning course you have a great deal of freedom. Can you think of some of the advantages and disadvantages of this freedom for you?

How are you going to use the 'freedom to learn' which you have as an adult? How are you going to make your learning meaningful to you?

How are you going to make sure that your learning is not simply 'knowledge for knowledge's sake' but is relevant to the other parts of your life?

Are you still carrying any 'baggage' about studying, left over from your school days? If so, what are you going to do about it?

A time to learn

This chapter will help you to think about the time you need to study and how to manage that time so that you use it to the full. It will also help you to think about where you are going to study and how to set up the right sort of environment. By the end of this chapter you will have planned when you will study, set yourself some targets and thought about the effects of this on your family and work commitments.

Contents

The juggling act

Sometimes life can feel like a constant juggling act. There are so many hoops to keep in the air, and most of us end up dropping the occasional one! And now you are a student on a learning programme! It may feel as if there is just one more plate to keep spinning.

Even if you have studied a lot before, you might not have done so as an adult at home. Being a full-time student away from home with few domestic pressures or commitments is one thing. Studying at home is quite different. Pressure on your time comes from a number of sources:

- your family and friends

- your employment

- the practical tasks of life

- your church commitments

- your hobbies

- space for yourself

and now.....

- your new course of study

Write down the 12 most important things that you have to juggle with:

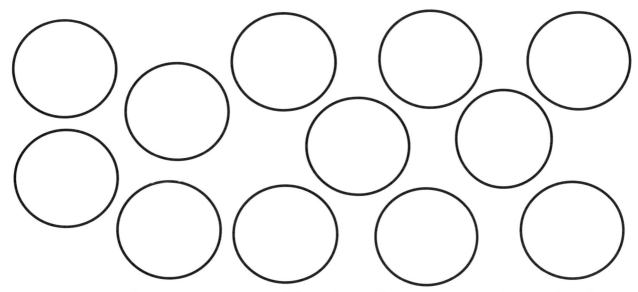

Does it look as if you're in danger of dropping a few hoops? How do you feel about your current load'?

No one can do everything. When you take on something new it often means letting go of something else. Take another look at your hoops. Try to think about priorities. You might like to number the items, giving number 1 to the person/task which seems to be to the most important and 2 to the next and so on.

If you manage to do this you may begin to see what it may be time to drop – not by accident but by design. No one has the same priorities throughout their lives. Situations change. Young dependent children grow into independent adults, the new job becomes familiar and so on.

Even commitments at church can and sometimes should change. It might just be time to realise that you are not indispensable to God's work in a particular situation.

What is becoming more important in your life?

What is becoming less important in your life?

How far can you see these changes as God prompting you to move on to new things?

How much time?

You might already have tried to make some assessment of how much time you need for study. Study units in St John's Extension Studies provide an average of 200 hours of study for a typical student with no previous experience of Higher Education. Being realistic, you cannot expect to complete such a unit in less than four months. That is nearly 15 hours a week – every week. Unless there is outside pressure on you requiring you to go at this pace, you might be better to settle for 7-10 hours a week. Of course, if you have more time available, you can always increase this rate, but beware of setting yourself impossible targets.

In order to study effectively......you need time

You need to stop and think more about what you actually do with your time now. Most of us can only plan ahead in a detailed way for a week at a time – so let's start there. You may not have such a thing as an average week but somehow or other you are going to have to work out the time you have free to study.

On the opposite page you will find a weekly planner. Block out and label all the times taken up with the events or activities that you do in a normal week. Include everything from sleeping to meals, watching TV, being at work, domestic chores and hobbies.

So how many spare hours do you have in an average week?

HOURS FREE FOR STUDY ....

Is that going to be enough? If not, you are going to have to make some changes and create some new time.

Here are some questions to help you review your weekly commitments:

- Do you really want to watch that much TV? Is much of it 'passive viewing'?

- Do you need quite that much sleep? Many students find that their most productive time is either first thing before anyone else is around, or late at night. (But don't overdo this – sleep is generally a good thing!)

- Have you thought of all the reading time there is on the train, or the bus, or while food is cooking?

- How do you feel about studying on Sunday? This is a decision only you can make.

- Do you need to reassess your church commitments? Your church should also benefit from your studies in the longer term. Is anyone taking that into account? Perhaps you should talk to your minister about this.

- Have you involved your family/ domestic partner/ friends in your assessment? Are the decisions you are making unilateral? Are others being genuinely supportive?

- Don't forget what 'all work and no play' does – everyone needs leisure time in a week.

My major problem in organising enough time to study seems to be:

I need to change the following in order to fit in study time:

At first sight all this planning might seem like time wasted when you could be studying, but it is far more likely to ensure that you have the time to study each week and that you can use the rest of the week to the full.

My week at a glance

Time	Sun	Mon	Tues	Wed	Thurs	Fri	Sat
1am							
2am							
3am							
4am							
5am							
6am							
7am							
8am							
9am							
10am							
11am							
noon							
1pm							
2pm							
3pm							
4pm							
5pm							
6pm							
7pm							
8pm							
9pm							
10pm							
11pm							
midn't							

Go with the flow

Finding the time to study can be difficult. You have other people's needs to consider along with your own. Very few people have many days when they are completely free to please themselves. Perhaps you have a number of set commitments each day. If your life is very full, then it is easy to fall into the trap of seeing your commitments as obstacles in the way of your study. Life soon becomes 'one long obstacle race'.

You have to go with the flow of your life rather than fight against it. You have to fit your study time around the commitments of your life. Look for reliable slots of time each week, rather than always trying to carve them out here and there. You may find that it is better to look for shorter slots of time and use them, rather than wait in hope for vast acres of time, which in reality will never appear.

In planning your weekly timetable don't overdo the study sessions. Build in breaks and reward yourself when you achieve your target.

The flow of a year

Going with the flow over a year is also important. For many there are natural 'good' times to take up new projects. For example, the beginning of a new academic year is a good time to start studying, as the evenings are drawing in.

Most of us have busy and not so busy times during a year. There are holidays to fit in and big family occasions. If you have school age children then there may be problems in trying to work during the school holidays. There may be times in the year when your work situation is particularly pressurised.

Some people cannot study for a particular length of time each week. You may need to think in blocks of time – whole days and even weeks spent in study, with periods in between when no study is done at all.

Starting a new job, moving house or having a baby can disrupt life for quite a while and it is probably unrealistic to expect to get much study done for quite a few months. In such situations it is better to be realistic from the start rather than struggle on feeling that you really ought to be studying but never getting down to it.

Q. How long does it take to have a good idea?
A. A holiday.

Susan gets home from work at 6 pm. She has a quick meal and aims to get down to study by 6.45 pm. She often finds it difficult to get started but tries to keep going until 10.30. She does this two nights a week but admits that the study is becoming a bind.

Your advice:

CASE STUDIES

Consider these three students. How effective do you think each of them is in planning their study time? What advice would you give to them about how they could improve things for themselves?

"Distance learning is that form of education which yields to the life-cycle of the student and does not destroy or prevent his productive relations to society" (Ross Kinsler)

Alan took early retirement but now works for the local church in a voluntary capacity most mornings until noon. He fits in a short study session before lunch, and then spends two afternoons a week studying – starting at 1.30 pm and finishing at 3.00 pm in order to pick up his wife from her church meeting. He always breaks for a cup of tea around 2.15.

Your advice:

Eileen has two teenage children. She is a qualified teacher but doesn't work outside the home at present. There never seems to be enough time for everything. There are all the household chores, like the ironing, to do and the children are always bringing friends home or need her to be their taxi service. She tries to sit down to study but can never concentrate for long – there is always so much to do. Eileen finds assignments virtually impossible and often gets low marks; this discourages her because she used to be able to do things really well.

Your advice:

My advice for the students on the previous page:

Susan is clearly suffering from mental (and probably physical) indigestion! It would be much better to take a longer break before starting study. I admire her stamina but I really wonder how effective this very long period of study time is. A break half way through and some relaxation time afterwards would also help. Yes, I have cut down her study time but I expect what she does will be more effective. She might also try to spread the load over three evenings instead of two.

Alan seems to have got things pretty well organised. In many ways his life is easier because he is retired but see how the pattern could also work for a mum with children at school.

Eileen is quite capable of doing the course in spite of lots of problems here. Could other members of the family help out? How about organising the morning by putting study first, then do the ironing, then the shopping?

The counter flow

It would be naive to think you can fit everything in just by going with the flow of life. Sometimes we have to swim against the tide. We have to take account of the legitimate demands of family and work, and feel the 'force' of these parts of our life as they work in tension with our opportunity for study.

What are the 'currents' you will have to swim against?

•

•

•

•

•

•

•

Stilling the storm

Life is full of tensions and it is important to recognise the legitimate tensions in our lives. But it is equally important for everyone's well-being to make sure that tensions don't develop into conflicts.

You may have already begun to think about how others could help you 'find' the time to study. Perhaps someone else could cook tea or pick up the children or lead the Bible study group? But if they are to do this, it may mean that they will be making sacrifices on your behalf. How will you and the other people involved feel about that? Will you need to compensate them in some other way?

Some of us find it very difficult to ask for, and receive, someone's gift to us of their time and energy. The decision to study may mean that you have to learn to receive as well as to give.

Asking for and receiving help will be important in your learning. It will be necessary to keep the channels of communication open between you and those who are willing to help you.

Targeting your time

All these students have problems using their study time. What about you? How are you going to spend the study time you have created for yourself?

"Some weeks I seem to get through loads of work and in others....well, I hardly get anything done."

"I really don't work well under the pressure of a deadline. I always leave things until it is too late and then have to rush it."

"I can't seem to settle down to work. I can never decide what I ought to do first."

"I do my six hours per week very religiously but don't seem to be getting anywhere."

Set the target

You can't score a bull's-eye unless you have a bull's-eye to aim at! And you will never have a sense of achievement at the end of a study session unless you knew what you wanted to achieve in the first place.

Planning your study session is an important key to successful learning. Here are some of the tasks you might want to do in a study session. As you get into the course you will soon find that you can plan each study time by setting yourself targets.

LEARNING TASKS
- read the next section in the unit course book
- make notes on part of a text book you have been asked to read
- sort out and file notes
- gather notes and ideas for an assignment
- watch a required video/DVD or listen to a cassette

You may find that half an hour spent at the beginning of the week setting yourself targets for each study session during that week means that you save a lot of time later on. It is important to realise that you will only be able to do this effectively once you have developed ideas about how much time you need for each particular type of task. For example, if you only have a half hour study period then it probably isn't going to be worth starting to read and take notes on a long and detailed chapter of a book. The half hour would probably be better spent doing a more limited task, such as filing recent notes.

At the end of each week it is important to look back and see how well you kept to the timetable. Don't worry if you didn't keep to it. The important thing to ask is why you didn't keep to it. Was it too ambitious? Was there an emergency/crisis that threw everything? Whatever the reason, learn from it and work those ideas into the timetable for the next week.

Take aim

Sometimes the work you will do as a student is very broadly defined. For example, you might be told to go away and research a subject for an assignment. There may be little guidance about which books to read or how long you should spend on the task. This will mean that you are left to make a lot of decisions about the nature and requirements of the task. What should you do?

You can break such a task down into a number of smaller, more manageable targets. You can then focus in on each one of these and plan when you can do them. If you have been asked to research a subject for an assignment you could break the task down in the following way:

• Go to the library to get some books
• Read relevant chapters
• Take notes
• Gather notes together, pick out relevant information for the assignment
• Make a plan of the assignment
• Write first draft of the assignment
• Write the assignment.

Once your target is well-focused, you need to make sure that you have all the things you need to get down to work. Preparing to study is important. You need to get yourself in the right mind-set. Perhaps you could think about the task you want to tackle as you walk the dog or drive home from work.

There are a number of other ways of preparing for a study period. Here are just a few hints:

• If you have lots of little things to do – make a coffee, a phone call, or find a pen – do it before the start of your study session, so that you don't have to keep stopping.

• If you have a video, programme it before you start studying otherwise you will be tempted to stop to watch your favourite TV serial.

• Let everyone in the house know that you are now studying and do not want to be disturbed.

Fire!

No-one ever hits the target unless they fire the arrow! The best way of starting a study session is to stop planning it and to get started! How long you work for before you have a break is very much a personal decision. People have different concentration spans but it is probably worth having a break after 90 minutes.

You may find that your work book or course notes tell you exactly what you are required to do and describe each task in neat, clear-cut terms. You may also find that you are given some kind of guidance about the time you should spend on a certain section. Any guidance on the amount of time you should take is only an average. You may take a longer or shorter amount of time to complete the work.

Working at home? — a cautionary tale

Susan had finally got the kids off to bed. She made herself a cup of coffee and then sat down in the lounge determined that tonight she would read and take notes on a section in a textbook. She was tired and fancied reading in a comfy chair.

It took her quite a while to get into the book, especially as the TV was right in her line of vision and she knew there was a good programme on, which she would really have liked to watch.

After reading a couple of pages Susan realised that there was some really good material here for her next assignment and that she needed to make notes as she went along. She got up, found a pen and paper and settled down again. It was difficult to make notes whilst sitting in the comfy chair.

Her husband then arrived home from work. They had already agreed that on the evenings when Susan was studying he would get his own meal.

Susan was now getting into the chapter of the book quite well. Her husband was very happy to help by getting his own tea and doing all the washing up but resented not being able to sit down in front of the TV afterwards. After some heated discussion Susan got up and went to work in the other room. It was cold in the other room and Susan felt angry – it was almost impossible to settle down to work again.

Fifteen minutes later a friend from church came round to discuss organising a family service. He only really needed to see her husband, but Susan heard the friend arrive and as she felt quite strongly about the subject they were discussing, had half an ear on the discussion and was paying very little attention to her reading. Ten minutes later Susan's husband came in to ask her advice about the music for the service. Susan gave up, went back into the warm lounge and planned the family service.

Why was Susan's attempt at study bound to fail? What advice would you have given her? (My ideas are over the page)

Assuming you decide that home is where you want to work, what are the things you ought to consider?

Susan's tale of woe

Susan's study session (previous page) failed for a number of reasons:

1. She was tired.
Perhaps this wasn't the best time of the day to work. If the children are at school perhaps she could have worked earlier on in the day.

2. She chose to sit in a comfy chair
and it was difficult to make notes. Comfy chairs are sleep-inducing. To study effectively most people need a table and an upright chair, even just to read something.

3. There were too many temptations
and distractions. Many people find it helpful to establish a place where they regularly to do their studying – a place they associate with study. Moving around the house isn't always helpful – although with a family it is sometimes necessary. Perhaps they have a spare bedroom where Susan could have a chair and desk.

4. Susan didn't have the equipment she needed
beside her. To study effectively you need to have everything you need close at hand. Perhaps the books you are using need to be on a nearby shelf, pens and paper on the desk.

5. Well done to Susan and her husband
for discussing the meal arrangements! Susan's husband had made an effort to support her in her studying. Susan might have anticipated that her husband would want to watch TV and started her study session in the other room. She could then have made sure the room was at the right temperature.

6. The visitor was not for Susan
and she could already have decided that in her own mind. She could have let friends know that on a particular night she would be studying – that way she would not have felt embarrassed at keeping out of the way, and her husband and friend would not have consulted her.

Time or task?

In this chapter we have been looking at time management (how you find the time to study) and task management (what you do when you study). You need to balance both. Some people tend to become obsessed with time – the hours they have put in. The problem here is that quantity is not always enough – you need quality as well. (How long does it take to have a good idea?) Just filling up the time with unimportant tasks is not going to get anyone very far. On the other hand some people get obsessed with the task – getting the assignment finished however long it takes. You can take too much time over a piece of work. Learning how to balance these two perspectives comes with experience – but for now, just try to keep them both in mind.

Home
or away?

So you have the time. And you know what you want to achieve. But where do you get down to doing it? Choosing the right place to study is important. You need to be somewhere you are not going to be distracted. You will also need somewhere to keep your course material and other equipment.

So think now about:

• where you are going to study.

• what action you need to take to ensure that you won't be disturbed.

• what the effect of this will be on those you live with and how you might compensate for this.

It may be relatively easy for you to study at home and not be disturbed. But equally you may never be alone in the house and cannot get a minute to yourself. Perhaps you get a lot of visitors coming to the door, and while you may enjoy being able to see others while you work, you need to weigh up whether you might get more done by being alone. The telephone and the doorbell can destroy a study session, if we let them. It is nice to feel wanted, and I know how guilty I get when I ignore them. But what would the caller have done if I was out shopping? If you can't cope with the idea of someone coming to your door and being ignored, leave a note outside!

There are advantages in studying from home as you can have all your materials to hand but there are alternatives you might like to consider.........

What about....

• The local library?

• Your workplace – perhaps you could get permission to arrive early or leave late?

• Is there someone living locally with a spare room who could make it available to you to study in without interruptions? You might be wise to check out whether everyone in your host's house agrees with this!

Wandering eyes?

Wherever you are, remember that the Lord is with you. Your studies are not remote from him. You might like to put a text on your pinboard or have a cross or another symbol on your desk to remind you, as your eyes wander, that your studies are as much a part of your walk with God as any other activity.

Pick up the crumbs!

There are often times when you find yourself at a loose end. Waiting for the take-away, or the bus. Stuck in a traffic jam, waiting in the doctor's surgery. If you know there is going to be a wait take something with you to read or some notes that you want to review. Don't tell yourself that you can't study just because it is not one of your usual places. Make these times work for you.

Getting organised

As with any task, you will study and learn better if you have the appropriate basic equipment. Here is a list of some of the things you might need. Put a tick against any you think you will need to purchase. (WHSmith's are not paying me commission!)

• writing paper – preferably A4 size
• A4 ring binder or cardboard wallet
• stapler or paper clips – notes soon get out of order
• filing box to contain all your course material
• a notebook
• pencil and pen
• a highlighter pen
• shelf or box for storing reference books

• pinboard – facing your desk with your planners pinned onto it and other reminders
• a lamp – an angle-poise one is a good idea if you are studying in the evenings
• a thick woolly jumper or a heater to keep you warm when you are sitting still.

Whenever you start something new there is always a temptation to buy too much. Try to think green! A cardboard box from the supermarket will do just as well as a pretty coloured one from the stationer's. How about recycled paper? Care for creation – God loves it and so should we!

What about books?

There are three kinds of books you are likely to need for a distance learning course.

1 The first is 'essential reading' – you literally cannot do the course without these. Mostly these are worth having on your book shelf for the future, so worth buying rather than borrowing.

2 The second kind of book is 'further reading'. Don't rush out and buy these unless you are sure you want them. Also try public libraries, or your minister's book shelves, or someone who has done the course before.

3 The third type is 'reference books'. These might include:

· A Study Bible (like The New Revised Standard Version or The New International Version. There are special study versions of these translations)
· A Bible Atlas
· A Theological Dictionary
· A one-volume Bible Commentary

...and computers?

While plenty of people are still happy to live without them, computers can be of enormous benefit if you have an assignment to write. The following guidelines will help you if you choose to use the computerised approach:

Choose a name for your document early on ('Save as...') and save it in a folder where you can find it. Then make sure you save it regularly as you input the text. To be on the safe side, keep a back-up copy on floppy disk or CD rom each time you pack away.

Find out the particular requirements of your course as regards referencing, line-spacing and front sheets. Don't try to use gimmicks in the layout. Your tutor will thank you for keeping your assignment as plain as possible, so don't be tempted to use more than one font, the easier to read the better. Left justification is easier to read than text that is justified on the right as well, because the spaces are consistent.

If your tutor is happy to receive your assignment by email (check first!), print out a copy to read through yourself before sending it. Somehow mistakes can be easy to miss onscreen.

Learn to use the word-count - a very useful tool. The spell-checker can also be handy, but BEWARE of being too dependent on it. Remember that it is designed for American English, so it may tell you that perfectly good English spellings (eg 'colour') are misspelt. In addition, it will not pick up as wrong any word that actually exists - even if it is far removed from the one you intended to use. The person who sent in a job application accompanied by a sheet headed "Cirrocumuli Vitae" had a few lessons to learn about using her spellchecker!

Another useful feature is the 'Header and footer' option. If you can master it, it helps the tutor if you can number your pages, and maybe even add a header to each page with your name and the assignment number.

So now you are ready to fill in your study planner - your new life with built-in study times. Have a go!

It's your time!

	Morning	Afternoon	Evening
Sun			
Mon			
Tues			
Wed			
Thur			
Fri			
Sat			

There will be some weeks when you get very little or nothing done. Thinking ahead will mean that you may be able to make up the hours you lose at other times. Mark on the year planner below all your known big commitments – holidays, school holidays, family events, busy times at work and so on. Allow the time you need to prepare for events like holidays, and the sorting out afterwards. When you have done this try to find some weeks when you might be able to fit in some extra hours.

	1	2	3	4	5	6	7	8	9	10	11	12	13	14	15	16	17	18	19	20	21	22	23	24	25	26	27	28	29	30	31
Jan																															
Feb																															
Mar																															
Apr																															
May																															
Jun																															
Jul																															
Aug																															
Sep																															
Oct																															
Nov																															
Dec																															

Now learn to read!

Students are often worried about the speed at which they read and take in material. This chapter will help you to think about some of the ways in which you could improve your reading skills so that you learn more effectively.

Contents

Styles of
reading

We spend a lot of our time in adult life reading. We read newspapers, magazines, novels, road signs, bus timetables, instruction manuals, recipe books, memos at work, and so on. But we don't read all these things in the same way.

Consider how you would approach reading a bus timetable and then compare it with how you would read a novel. How would you describe the difference?

Most people don't spend ages going through every page of a timetable. We find the appropriate page and then ignore all the rest. If you tried approaching reading a novel in that way you'd soon lose some of the enjoyment and probably never get to grips with the plot.

Light reading

This is the reading you do beside the swimming pool when you are on holiday! It is also the sort of reading you do when you read a magazine or newspaper article. I normally associate this type of reading with reading for pleasure. Often people read quite quickly and perhaps retain very little of the information in the following weeks or months.

It would be wrong to say that you will never use this type of reading when you are studying. It is a useful way into many of the books of the Bible. To sit down and read through an Old Testament historical book or a Gospel can give you a very useful overall view of the writer's interests and intentions.

In this chapter reference is made to Introducing the New Testament by John Drane (Lion Publishing, 1999). A copy of this book is not essential for understanding the contents of the chapter but will be necessary for some of the exercises. If you are not able to get hold of a copy it is still possible to set yourself similar tasks using another textbook.

We read different kinds of books in different ways. Those who read effectively choose different methods of reading for different tasks.

Scanning

Scanning is the rapid search for a key point or word. It is the sort of reading you do when you look up a number in a telephone directory. This kind of reading is useful when you are looking up a subject in the index of a book or on the contents page.

You might also use a scanning technique once you have turned to a page referred to in the index. Often there is little point in reading the whole page. What you need is to find the word you are looking for and then read the sentences around it and perhaps the paragraphs on either side.

Use J. Drane's Introducing the New Testament. Give yourself two minutes to find references to 'Porcus Festus'. Do this without reading whole pages of text.

Do the same with 'Emperor Caligula'.

Skimming

Previewing or skimming is essential if you are going to use books effectively in your study programme. Previewing helps you decide if a book is relevant to the area you are studying. It then helps you decide which bits of a book to read and study in greater depth. When you are previewing or skimming through a book you might look at:

• **table of contents:** usually on the first couple of pages, listing chapter headings
• **index:** normally found at the end of the book, presenting items in alphabetical order
• **chapter summaries:** found at the beginning of each chapter or in the table of contents. Not all books have these.
• **sub-headings:** found in the main text of chapters
• **first and last paragraphs of chapter:** often introduce and sum up what has been said.

When you have skimmed a book in this way, you will know which sections are appropriate to your needs and won't need to waste time reading all the rest (unless you then decide that the whole of the book is relevant to your needs).

You have been asked to write an essay on 'The understanding of Jesus as portrayed in the Fourth Gospel'. Which section of Drane's Introducing the New Testament would you certainly have to read for this essay?

Word by word

Some passages in some books need to be read a word at a time. Everyone needs to employ this technique at some time. Consider this sentence in a book on modern culture, *Hiding the Light* by D. Hebdige (Routledge 1988 page 187): For most people this sentence contains a number of unfamiliar words. This means

> *Beneath the euphemistic masks of, for instance, 'disinterested Reason', 'scientific Marxism', 'objective' statistics, 'neutral' description, 'sympathetic' ethnography or 'reflexive' ethnomethodology, the eye of the Post is likely to discern the same essential 'Bestiary of Powers' (see, especially, Jean Baudrillard and Paul Virilio for explicit denunciation of 'sociology').*

that we have to stop and let our eye take in each new word. We may also need to dissect the word and work out how it might be pronounced. We may try looking the word up in a dictionary. Then, once we have got some idea of the meaning, we

have to go through a process of mental re-writing. This will involve trying to work out the meaning of the sentence as a whole. It is often important to take extensive notes when we are reading this type of material. In fact, note-taking helps a great deal in the process of mental re-writing.

As we become more experienced readers, the number of times we need to pause like this over words will gradually diminish but it will never disappear altogether. Whenever we start a new subject, there are always going to be a number of words we haven't met before. Some of these will be unique to the subject that we are studying. Other words – such as 'validity', 'erroneous' and 'elucidate' – may be unfamiliar to you but are commonly used in 'academic' books. This is where a good dictionary is a great help. You will find a glossary of common theological terms at the back of this book.

Reading to learn

This is the type of reading which is slow and repetitive. You are aiming to 'take in' the major facts and ideas, and understand the arguments in a text. In other words, you are reading with a purpose. Reading is a way of developing your thoughts as well as providing you with new ideas and information. Thinking is a big part of reading to learn. You will learn as you read when you engage with the ideas you are presented with and rethink your own.

Although it is sometimes necessary to use the other types of reading outlined above to study effectively, most of the textbook reading you will be doing will be 'reading to learn'. We will look at reading to learn in more detail in this chapter.

You will find the answers to the exercises on these pages on page 38 .

Now read through the article on 'Miracle Stories in the Gospels' on the next two pages. Read it quite quickly and don't take any notes. Make a note of how long it takes you to read the passage.

These pages are adapted from John Drane: *Introducing the New Testament* (1986 ed.) pages 139-141, used by kind permission of Lion Publishing

Miracle Stories in the Gospels

It is when we come to the Gospels themselves that we encounter some of the most formidable problems about Jesus' miracles. Three main questions need to be considered here.

Jesus' ability to heal became so well known that crowds followed him wherever he went. Healing services and medical missions have remained an important part of Christian activity.

• Some form critics, scholars who study how the Gospels were written, have shown that in their literary form the miracle stories of the Gospels are often similar to stories found in Hellenistic literature. A number of scholars have drawn particular attention to the parallels between the Gospel accounts and the stories of a first-century Cappadocian seer and wonder-worker found in the *Life of Apollonius,* written by the third century author Philostratus. This of course is what we might expect, for the stories of Jesus' miracles were first written down by Greek-speaking people, who would naturally use the literary forms and conventions that were most familiar to them. It is hardly surprising that authors writing about the same kind of incidents in the same cultural situation should use similar language.

In addition, the 'parallels' drawn between Apollonius and Jesus favour the originality of the Gospel traditions. Not only are the Hellenistic stories of much later date than the New Testament, but they were published with the express purpose of disputing the Christian claims about Jesus. If there is any question of 'dependence' by either account on the other, it could more easily be supposed that later writers consciously modelled their stories on the Gospel accounts than the other way round. In any case, similarity of literary form can really tell us nothing at all about the historical facts. (See the fuller discussion in chapter 10).

• It is a well known fact of history that as time goes on, miracles tend to be attached to people who are highly regarded for other reasons. We can see this tendency at work in the legends that have been gathered around the lives of so many of the medieval saints. It is undeniable that the same thing happened to the stories of Jesus. We can see this from the so-called 'apocryphal gospels' which were written in the second century. They relate all kinds of bizarre miracle stories about Jesus. There are also certain miracle stories in the New Testament Gospels of Matthew and John that some have compared with the stories in these apocryphal gospels. But on the whole there is compelling evidence to suggest that the central miraculous element of the New Testament Gospels does not derive from this kind of speculation. In the first place, according to some recent datings of the Gospels, the earliest written records about the life of Jesus may be as early as AD45, which is only fifteen years after his death. E ven the more conventional dating of Mark to about AD65-70 takes us only thirty-five years beyond the events recorded in the Gospels. A conscious mythologizing process would certainly need longer than that to develop, and at the time the Gospels were taking shape there must have been many surviving eye-witnesses of the events they describe. They could no doubt have corrected any stories that were out of character with Jesus as they remembered him.

Then there is also a striking difference between the miracle stories of the New Testament Gospels and the stories told about Hellenistic "divine men". or medieval saints, or even about Jesus himself in the apocryphal gospels. There is, for example, nothing in the New Testament to compare with the grotesque tale told in the *Arabic Infancy Gospel*, according to which Jesus produced three children out of some goats he found in an oven. And even the story found in the *Infancy Gospel of Thomas* about Jesus turning twelve clay birds into real sparrows on the sabbath is of quite a different character from the stories told in the New Testament. Legendary tales of miracles are almost always concerned with the ostentatious display of special powers. But in the four Gospels there is none of this. Indeed it is made quite clear that the miracles Jesus performed were not concerned with satisfying idle speculation about the supernatural. When the Pharisees asked Jesus to perform a miracle to satisfy their curiosity, he told them in no uncertain terms that this kind of spectacle was quite alien to his work (Matthew 12:38-42; Mark 8:11-12; Luke 11:29-32).

It is also significant that Jesus is portrayed as a worker of miracles in even the very earliest strands of the Gospel traditions that we can trace. The Gospel course Q (see chapter 10) is generally thought to have been an early collection of Jesus' sayings, but this material also reports one miracle, the healing of the Roman centurion's servant (Matthew 8:5-13; Luke 7:1-10). It also states that Jesus was in the habit of doing miracles. It is in Q that John's disciples are told to report the miracles they have seen (Matthew 11:1-19; Luke 7:18-35), and the cities of Galilee are condemned because they have not repented in spite of the miracles done in them (Matthew 11:20-24; Luke 10:13-15).

Perhaps the strongest reason for distinguishing the Gospel miracles from both pagan and later Christian stories is the fact that in the New Testament the miracles mean something. They are not just demonstrations of the supernatural for its own sake. Rather they are an essential part of Jesus' message about the arrival of God's new society.

• There is, however, yet another aspect. It is often pointed out by sceptics that in at least two of his temptations Jesus decisively rejected the temptation to perform miracles (Matthew 4:1-11; Luke 4:1-13). He was tempted to turn stones into bread and to throw himself from the temple without injury, and he refused to do either. Is it then likely that he would perform in the course of his ministry such a miracle as the feeding of the 5000, which apparently resulted in the crowd trying to make him their king? (See John 6:1-15; Matthew 14:13-21; Mark 6:30-44; Luke 9:10-17).

This is not such a problem as it appears at first sight. Indeed it only arises if we regard Jesus first and foremost as a wonder-worker. The ancient world was full of magicians who practised their art as a means of displaying their own special powers and significance. But the whole tone of the Gospel stories is quite different. Jesus' work is characterized not by a quest for power, but by humble service of God and man. In the temptations he rejected the possibility of commanding the obedience of men and women by working wonders, and the Gospels show how even his miracles were subordinated to that intention. For the miracles, like his teaching and preaching, were a call for faith and obedience from those who experienced or witnessed them.

It seems therefore that the various pieces of evidence all have the same implication. Both Jewish and Christian sources suggest that Jesus did perform remarkable deeds. Though there is obviously room for making different judgements about different miracles, we cannot reasonably dispose of the whole of the miraculous element in the Gospel traditions. At the same time, we must resist the temptation to regard the miracles as an end in themselves. Like so many other parts of Jesus' ministry, their real significance lies in what they teach us about God.

Reading with a purpose

Cover the opposite page. Can you answer these questions on "Miracle Stories in the Gospels" without looking back to the article?

What were the three main questions needing consideration?

Answers to questions on pages 34 and 35
The references to Porcus Festus are on p348 (first paragraph) and 350 (left column first paragraph, as simply 'Festus'). Did you realise that you could look up the surname in the index?

The reference to Emperor Caligula is on p49 (bottom of first column and top of second).

What evidence or arguments are given to show that the miraculous element of the New Testament Gospels is not purely speculative?

The section you would need to read for an essay about the understanding of Jesus as portrayed in the fourth Gospel is on pp 208-216. The index was of little help here. What I did was to look at the contents page. I found a chapter called 'Four portraits of Jesus' with a section on John. That sounded hopeful but I skimmed through the section to make sure it gave me the kind of information I wanted.

What place do the miracles have in the life of Jesus?

Now check your answers against mine on the opposite page.

My suggested answers *to the questions opposite:*

1. What were the main questions needing consideration?

It was easy to identify these by looking at the way the passage was laid out. Did you notice the three heavy dots? The three main questions were:

1. the relationship of the NT miracle stories with other Hellenistic literature
2. the adding of legendary type stories to the life of Jesus – what Drane calls a 'Mythologising process'
3. the role of miracles in Jesus' ministry.

2. What evidence/ arguments are given to show that the miraculous element of Jesus's life is not purely speculative?

If you had known about this question before you started to read you could have looked out for any mention of 'speculation'. It comes in the second section. Drane makes four points here:

1. the implications of the early date of the Gospels
2. the miracles Jesus is said to have performed are not like the typical legendary material found elsewhere.
3. the record of the miracles in the earliest documents/strands which go to make up the Gospels
4. the link between the miracles and the teaching of Jesus.

3. What place do the miracles have in the life of Jesus?

The answer to this is found in the last section of the extract. The miracles fit alongside Jesus' teaching and are a call to faith and obedience. They were not an end in themselves.

How did you do?

Did you manage to get them all? If you did then you did extremely well. Most people wouldn't have got all of them in detail after a simple reading of the passage and I certainly think I'd have struggled.

"The purpose of reading is not to have a lot of words pass in front of your eyes, nor to add a few new items to a long 'list' of information in your mind. It is to engage your ideas and make you rethink them."

Open University, *The Good Study Guide* p34

The reason why you struggled was that I made you read the passage without any purpose. I only asked you questions about the passage after you had read it (if you didn't cheat!) and that probably meant that you would have to go through the passage again to find the answers.

Imagine what it would have been like to read the passage for the first time with a set of questions already in your mind. You would have been able to look out for hints and even key words in the text. You would have been reading with a purpose. You would have been reading to learn.

SQ3R:
one method of reading

Survey

It is unlikely that in the initial stages of theological study you will be required to read a theological book from cover to cover at one time. But even if you are only asked to read a certain section, it repays you to get a good feel for the whole book by looking at the introductory pages and skimming through the chapter headings. Here are some things you might look for:

• **How does the bit you will read fit into the book as a whole?**

• **Are there other parts of the book that might be relevant to the subject?**

• **Who is the author? Do you know anything about the person? How might that prejudice you as you read their writings?**

• **Is it going to be a difficult book to read? Sample a paragraph. Is the style manageable? Are you going to have to set aside extra time to cope with it?**

If you are doing some independent research on a subject and think a book might be useful, it is also worth looking at:

• **The date of publication. Is it reasonably new; if not, is it out of date, has it been revised, is it popular (has it been reprinted)?**

• **Who was the book written for? Is it written at the right sort of level for the work you are doing? Was it written with a particular situation or culture in mind, and if so, how well will it translate to your own situation?**

Question

We have already seen how important it is when 'reading with a purpose' to approach the reading with particular questions in mind. Keep those specific questions in mind all the way through the reading.

At other times you may have to rely on more general questions, such as:

- **What is the main argument of this section?**
- **How do these ideas differ from other books I have read on the same subject?**
- **Do I agree with what is being said?**
- **Are there any useful points for my next assignment?**
- **Are there any useful quotations?**

Read

What you were really doing when you read the Drane passage on miracles was previewing or skimming. It is wise to do this before reading a passage or chapter in detail. Skimming will help you to see how the chapter divides up and what seem to be the important points or issues. When you have scanned the section you are reading, you are then ready to read the passage more slowly to pick out the detailed arguments.

At this point it is important that you enter into a conversation with the book, particularly if the author is airing some particular theories. You need to ask:

- **Is this argument fair?**
- **Is the evidence adequate?**
- **Do I agree?**
- **Is there another way of looking at all this?**

Remember

How do you propose to hold on to this new information? Does your reading go in one eye and out the other? Try to say out loud the main points of the chapter or paragraph. It is a good idea to make notes at this stage and I will say more about this in the next chapter.

Review

Check back over what you recall. Were there important points which you missed out? If necessary, you may need to amend your notes.

>>>> Now go to the foot of p46 for an exercise

Speeding it up

The passage from Drane on pages 36-37 is roughly 1000 words. How long did you take? And what was your speed?

 words per minute

It can seem as if there is a never-ending pile of reading to do and you may soon begin to wonder if you will ever be able to read it all. Some students then begin to worry about the speed at which they read.

How fast is **fast?**

Books on study skills will tell you about reading speeds (usually expressed as the number of words you can read in a minute). They may state what they think is a good reading speed for people who are studying. It is however very difficult to get a reliable indicator of the speed at which anyone reads and even more difficult to say at what rate a person should be reading. This is because the speed you read at is dependent on a lot of different factors. These may include:

The Open University give the following as a rough 'rule of thumb' for speeds:

Easy text; fairly familiar material: 100 words per minute

Moderately hard text which you want to follow closely: 70 words per minute

Difficult text; unfamiliar subject matter which you want to understand in depth: 40 words per minute

- whether the subject matter is familiar to you
  - how difficult the text is (vocabulary, lay-out etc.)
    - if you are interested in what you are reading
      - how thoroughly you need to understand the text.

There is never a 'right' amount of time to spend on reading something. You must first decide what you want to achieve from reading the passage and then allocate time appropriately.

Faster reading

There are some ways in which it is possible to improve the speed at which you read:

- Decide on your purpose before you start.
- Concentrate on the main ideas in the text.
- Skim the text first.
- If you know you have to look for some key concepts, scan the text for key words first.
- If you read a sentence and find that you haven't understood it, don't go back immediately. Read on. The context might give you clues to the meaning of the difficult sentence. Only go back at the end of the section if you still haven't got the key ideas.
- Don't mouth the words. If you tend to do this, try to read faster than you can speak for a while.
- Read more! Practice improves speed better than anything else!

Faster thinking

Speed isn't everything. Remember that the purpose of reading is to develop your thoughts, to give you new information and help you to fit these new things into your existing framework of knowledge. A big part of reading is thinking. If you by-pass the thinking bit you won't be learning.

You need to take the emphasis off the speed at which you read and consider the speed at which you think. You may learn to read faster but you may not be thinking faster and so you may not be learning faster. In fact, you may learn more quickly by reading more slowly.

Some people find that one way of overcoming this problem is to get into a pattern of reading a section quickly and then pausing for thought before going on again. Pausing for thought helps to keep the emphasis on the ideas you are reading about, rather than on simply reaching the end of what you are reading. You may like to try this pattern for yourself. You need to keep making decisions on your reading style, depending on what you need to learn. Sometimes it is worth investing a lot of time in reading a small section of a book, especially if that is central to the area you are studying. At other times it will be a waste of time to read in a very detailed way, and it is better to skim through several sections of a book or even several books.

Lay-by stops

We have all seen those signs on the motorway which read 'Tiredness Kills. Take a Break!' If you are planning a journey of two or three miles then it is sensible to drive straight there without any stops. But if you are planning a long journey it is wiser and safer to stop a couple of times on the way. We all recognise the danger of falling asleep at the wheel.

Reading a book is a bit like driving a car and you need to take similar precautions. Most people, at some time in their lives, have fallen asleep whilst reading a book. Often it is not because the book was boring but simply that we couldn't concentrate any longer. When planning reading time you must be realistic.

If you only have to read a small section of a book, then it is quite easy to allocate that to a particular study session during the week. But if you are asked to read a much longer chapter or section of a book, it is probably as well to divide the reading over a number of study sessions or at least give yourself a number of good long breaks!

Sticking points

Reading a text book is very different from reading a novel. The chances are you won't start at the beginning and work right through to the end. You will just 'dip' into certain bits. You will also notice that there are differences in the style of writing and if you haven't read this sort of book for a while then the style will take a bit of getting used to.

Some theological books are badly written and many assume a greater degree of knowledge than you already have. But persevere and you will soon get used to it. Actually, the more familiar you become with this academic style of writing the easier you will find it to write essays (although please don't make them as obscure as some theological books...). Here are some of the features you may find difficult.

New vocabulary

We have already noted the value of having a good dictionary. But stopping to look up every new word does slow up the reading process. You will need to decide if the word seems to be important. Does it keep coming up and is it stopping you understanding what is being said? A lot of new technical words can be off-putting but they are not put in to annoy you. Part of your learning is about coming into contact with new ideas and fitting new words to these ideas. Every subject has its technical vocabulary (even motor cycle maintenance – try looking at a repair manual!) and once you learn it it helps you 'handle' those ideas. A glossary of special words used in theological books is to be found at the end of this one. Keep it somewhere handy so that you can refer back to it.

Unfamiliar examples

What should you do when you don't understand everything you are reading because there are references made or examples used with which you are unfamiliar? You may begin to wonder if you should stop and find out about these. This is probably not a good idea. It might be worth making a note of any references you don't understand but it is probably not worth stopping to do any further research unless it is the subject of the passage you are reading. You can still get a lot out of the reading if you press on and try to get to grips with the main argument of the passage.

The subject doesn't appeal

In most distance learning courses you will be given precise sections of text books to read. This particular section may not appeal to you at all. If you do find that you are required to read something which you feel is irrelevant or boring, persevere. The writer might just draw you into the subject as you go along. If this doesn't get you going, try to set yourself a question. It might just be 'Why has the course writer asked me to read this?' Remember, the whole point of reading is that we learn something new and relate it to ideas we already have.

Academic style

It can be quite difficult to get used to 'text book style'. It often seems to take a long time for a point to be made and even when the point is made it is only made very cautiously. Phrases like 'It would seem then that the evidence indicates that there may well be...' abound.

This style is very different from the sort of things most of us read most of the time. In magazine articles and newspapers, points have to be made quickly and a certain stance or political line is often assumed from the start. This is not the case with an academic book. Nothing can be taken for granted and any point made must be capable of being shown to be true. The writer has to be as exact as possible and only say those things which can be justified.

This means that in academic books there is an argument being developed but it is done in an unemotional, detached and logical way. The academic world is also harsh on its members, and authors are often trying to protect themselves from criticism.

It's all rubbish!

Sometimes you will get annoyed with an author, particularly if they are going on and on about a point and you do not agree. You will want to stop and say 'Yes, but...'. And that is good because when we are studying our faith, it is impossible to be emotionally detached from what we are reading. This may especially be the case if you think that the author has a different view of Scripture from you and you are unhappy with the approach.

It is tempting in this situation to give up, but that would mean giving up learning too. No one is saying that you have to agree with a recommended author but if you only read things you agree with, then little learning will take place and you will never know how your views stand up to criticism. In fact, part of studying is about learning to cope with not feeling happy with what is being said and then carrying on to see how the argument develops. It may in fact be the case that the author was not saying what you had thought s/he was. Alternatively, if you still disagree with the author when you have finished the section you should try to use this disagreement in the learning process. When you disagree, try to write down why you disagree. Make a list of the author's points and match them with your counter-arguments point by point. That way you will come to grips with the text in an exciting way and develop your ability to put across an argument. This will stand you in excellent stead for later assignment writing.

EXERCISE

Try to remember as much as you can about 'reading with a purpose'. Write it down in note form in the 'Remember' box below. Then check to see if you remembered all the important points. If you missed any out, write them in the 'Review' box to emphasise them to yourself.

Remember	Review

You are not a disembodied mind, and your physical senses are important to your learning. We learn most efficiently by what we see. It will pay you to look after your eyes.

Is your eyesight good? When was the last time you had your eyesight checked? Do you need reading-glasses?

What angle is the reading matter in relation to your face? Some people like to use a book prop. (In fact the optimum position for reading a book is 90 degrees, although most of us have got into the habit of having the top of the book tilted away from us; but that is not ideal.)

Is there enough light without glare? Extremes of gloom or glare will give you eye-strain.

Eyes and ears

It is often assumed that people concentrate best when there is absolute silence. This may not, however, be the case. How do you feel about having background music while you work? If the idea appeals, try it out. It helps some people but distracts others.

Now carry on with p42

Feel like a sieve?

This chapter will help you to think about your ability to remember things, and ways in which you can "retain" things that are important. The chapter will consider the reasons for taking notes and help you to choose a method of note-taking that suits you. You will also have a chance to think about ways of storing notes and whether you wish to start writing a learning journal.

Contents

Dispelling the myths

How confident do you feel about your power to remember things? Perhaps, as you start a course of study, this is one area where you feel you are weak. But don't despair. Let's put a few things into perspective.

the memorisation myth

How did you feel when you first looked at your study materials? Did it feel like there was a lot to take in? Perhaps your immediate thought was 'How am I ever going to remember all this?'

The short answer is that nobody expects you to! To do well on a learning course you don't memorise the material. On many courses there are no assignments to be completed without the help of notes or books. In other courses there are exams or tests only on certain sections of the course. It is highly unlikely that you will ever be expected to take an unseen test on the whole of the course at any one time. The important thing will be not whether you

---

Many peoples (including the Jews) entrusted their entire cultural heritage and its survival to the memories of the very old.

---

have memorised the course material but whether you have learnt to use the course material effectively.

But you may well ask, 'What about the reading I have to do from the text books? What am I supposed to be able to remember from these?' You are not expected to memorise what you read. The chances are that even the author of the book wouldn't remember everything in the section you are reading. When authors have to re-read something they wrote earlier they often find ideas in it that they have forgotten they ever had. 'Did I really write that?' is a frequent response. If the author can't remember everything in their own book, you cannot be expected to either!

The point of reading something is not to be able to store the content in your mind and repeat it 'parrot-fashion' when asked. A parrot doesn't understand what it is saying, and learning something by heart does not show that you have understood what you have read. The point of reading a book is to gain new ideas and then go on and think with this new set of ideas. Whether you hold these ideas in your head or put them down in note form on paper doesn't really matter. The important thing is to find a method whereby you can retrieve these ideas for future use.

We all do it!

My father-in-law admits to having a bad memory. He tells a story of an occasion, soon after his marriage, when he was about to introduce his wife to a colleague. They were at an important social event and everyone was out to impress. My father-in-law began to introduce his wife: 'This is my wife… um… er… ' Panic ensued. What was her name? For what seemed like a century, but was probably only a few seconds, my father-in-law really couldn't remember his wife's name.

the **old-age** myth

A lot of things are said about age and memory. 'You can't teach an old dog new tricks' is one of the most frequently heard and most unflattering of sentiments. But is it really true? What is the relationship between age and memory?

The fact is that it is very difficult to generalise. Much of the research into memory tends to be very specific and loses all meaning when applied to people in general. Certainly, as we get older, some of the things we once found easy become less so. This is particularly true of physical skills. As I write this I have just been watching the Winter Olympics. Much of what I have seen has been thrilling but the harsh reality is that you have to be under the age of 25 to succeed. Competitors over that age had to work very hard to reach the top and often didn't make it.

There is some evidence that intellectual capacity can also decline with age, and research shows that this is particularly true about a person's memory of recent events. But we also know that this is much less true for people who keep themselves intellectually active. People who read, write and work with what they know are more likely to be able to hold things in their memories.

If you have a lively and enquiring mind your memory is not so likely to 'go' with age.

There are other reasons why it is assumed that age and memory don't go together. Studies have shown that when people are in situations where there is little change or challenge, learning does become harder. This is because the people involved become less flexible and find it hard to adapt. But it is one thing to recognise this and quite another to say that therefore all older people will find it difficult to take in new information. The truth is that whenever a person of any age faces little change or challenge, learning will be more difficult. And the fact that you are the sort of person who has been motivated enough to start a distance learning course would suggest that you do not fall into this category at all, or that you realise the danger of falling into it and have done something about it before it is too late!

the **history lesson** myth

You may remember finding it very difficult to memorise facts at school. History lessons have a particularly bad reputation here! Now that you are entering another learning situation, you may think, 'I was useless at school – why should it be any better now?'

If this is how you feel, consider why you didn't succeed at school. Were you anxious, bored or resentful? Perhaps you couldn't see any good reason for remembering what you were expected

to? Perhaps no one ever taught you how to remember things? Recall what we said in Chapter 1 about leaving school behind. The situation isn't the same and there is no reason why, with appropriate help, you shouldn't succeed now.

The more meaning something has for you, the more it is likely to remain with you. That's how it's different from school. Over the page you'll see how this works...

How your memory works

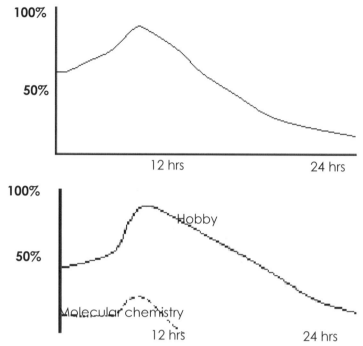

Look at the first graph. It shows the percentage of material you can expect to retain after different periods of time. Notice the points made below the graph.

The graph will vary according to the type of information that is being retained. Imagine you heard two lectures. One on molecular chemistry (my apologies if you find this subject fascinating…) and the other on a hobby which has interested you for many years. What do you think your graphs for each lecture would look like?

You don't need a degree in psychology to be able to study, but a little bit of knowledge of how your memory works will help you to learn more effectively.

Here is a diagram which illustrates how your memory works. You 'read' it from left to right. Information gets into your memory system by means of your senses. As you study the way information will enter is mostly through what you see (and through what you hear if you attend a lecture, listen to a cassette or watch a video).

Clearly, we don't take in everything we see, listen to, taste, smell and touch. A lot of information about the world we live in simply passes us by, or rather, we decide to pass it by. We 'sort' it.

Think back to the last time you walked through a busy street. You actually saw a lot of people – but how many faces can you recall? I suspect you can't remember any unless they were doing something which particularly drew your attention. We don't see or hear what we don't pay attention to, and we only partially see and hear when our attention is divided.

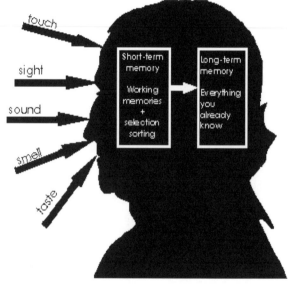

Read this list of words through once. Close the book and then see how many words you can write down. Then read my comments on the next page.

Doctrine	Roman
Matthew	Acts
Greek	Heresy
Eschatological	Luke
Mark	Jew
Creed	Romans
Hebrews	Faith
Synoptic	Samaritan

How did you get on?

Which words did you remember? Was 'eschatological' one of them? The chances are that it was, because it is unusual and stands out in the list because of its length.

Did you remember 'Doctrine' and 'Samaritan'? If you did, it is probably because those were the first and last words on the list. If your name is on the list you probably also noticed that one.

It is unlikely that you remembered more than seven of the words on the list. It seems that most people can only cope with learning seven 'chunks' of memory at one time.

Did you notice that it was possible to link the words together under themes?

- Words associated with the Gospels: Matthew, Mark, Luke, Synoptic, (Greek).
- Words associated with belief: Creed, Heresy, Faith, Doctrine.
- Words associated with NT books: Hebrews, Romans, Acts.
- Words associated with national groups: Samaritan, Jew, Roman, (Greek).
- Odd one out: Eschatological.

Would the words have been easier to learn if they had been set out like this? I suspect so.

> Forgetting is natural but it needn't be inevitable. There are ways of improving your memory so that you can retain the ideas that are important to you.

This exercise tells us quite a lot about things we find easy to remember. It seems that we remember best

- first and last things
- outstanding things
- familiar things
- linked things.

I would add one more thing to that list   • pictures of things.

Memory is a very complex process and the effectiveness of your memory also depends on general factors – two in particular:

Motivation
We learn when we are motivated. The more meaningful the material is to you, the easier it will be to remember. This should encourage you. Anyone who is motivated enough to apply and pay for a distance learning course shows a considerable amount of motivation!

Circumstances
The effectiveness with which you can cut off the rest of the world and concentrate on your studies will affect your learning. Equally, it is important to be relaxed. Tension interferes with short-term memory.

Short-term and long-term memory

The information we receive from our senses then passes into short-term memory. Psychologists cannot agree about the precise nature of the short-term memory. Some see it as a system designed to cope with items that don't need to be kept for long – like phone numbers which we look up in a directory and retain for the 30 seconds needed to dial them. Others see the short-term memory as a waiting room for long-term memory. They say that a selection process takes place and some things get passed on to long-term memory whilst other items are discarded. Perhaps you sometimes think your memory is like a sieve, but that, according to this theory, is exactly what it is. Your short-term memory is sifting outs bits of significant information and letting the rest drift away. The skill is to hold on to the really important stuff, and not fill up your memory with useless facts!

Your long-term memory is everything you know up to now. It is a mass of very complicated networks and links. Some of the knowledge in our long-term memories will only be a few minutes old; other bits of it will be as old as we are.

The point of reading is to be able to understand what you read and to be able to get back the ideas at some future point when you need them again. Holding them in your mind is by no means the only way. You can often construct a much more reliable route back to ideas you have been reading about by making notes.

The Good Study Guide, The Open University, p39

Write yourself a note

When was the last time you had to take some notes? At school – in order to pass an examination or because the teacher couldn't think of any other more interesting type of homework? Or maybe more recently – for a meeting or a talk you were giving?

On these occasions there might have been some good reasons for making notes. But what about now as part of your study on a distance learning course? Is note-taking important? I would argue that there are good reasons for taking notes.

1. Notes help you remember

Isn't this why we write shopping lists and have pin boards in the kitchen with notes written in huge letters on them? When we're in a mad rush or when we are trying to juggle lots of different things in our lives, notes jog our memory. No one can remember the entire contents of a book they read some time ago. Notes will help you to reconstruct what you have read. Notes also focus your attention, help you to concentrate and so help you remember what you have read.

2. Notes help you think

Making notes forces you to think about what you have read and then to put this down in a different form which makes sense to you. Notes are your way of explaining what you have read. Good note taking is not simply copying out part of the text. Note taking is about trying to summarise what you have read. It is looking for and recording the main points of an article or argument. Notes help you reorganise what you have learnt in a way that suits you. As you do this you are taking the information in and processing it at a deeper level.

3. Notes are a symbol of progress

If you read a book in a study session it may be difficult to see exactly what you have achieved at the end of the session. In a couple of weeks the chances are that you will have forgotten how you spent that study session and bemoan your lack of progress. Notes provide you with some evidence of the work you did. A good clear set of notes will help boost your morale when things don't seem to be moving very quickly.

4. Notes help you prepare

There is nothing worse than being faced with an assignment and knowing that you read about that topic somewhere but you can't quite remember where. Taking notes saves you having to flick through all the books you have read recently (!) to find where the topic was mentioned. Equally, if the assignment asks you to write on a totally new subject, taking notes will help you to draw together all the new reading you do as part of constructing the assignment.

Good practice in note-taking

There is no one right way of taking notes and it is important to find a way that suits you. There are however simple practices that will help in the note-taking process.

- **Legibility:** Can they be read not only now, but in a year or two?

- **Clarity:** Are they capable of more than one interpretation, or even worse, is it going to be possible to work out what they are about at all?

- **Suitability:** Do they meet your needs? Are they organised in a way that helps you to learn?

- **Brevity:** Are they over-specific and too detailed for the purpose you had in mind? Or do they lack enough detail to spark your brain into remembering the fuller argument?

Taking notes from books

Record the page numbers when you are taking notes from a book. For example, you might put at the top of a page of notes 'Drane – pp .30-33'.

Recording that much information will be quite adequate if you are only working from one or two books which have been recommended as part of the course. If you are reading more widely and using books which are not specifically recommended then it is a good idea to record:
- the title
- the author
- the publisher
- the date of that edition (latest © date)
This information will be important for any bibliography that you have to write for an assignment and will also be helpful for your tutor in assessing your work.

Where to write your notes

There are many possibilities:
- A4 paper kept in a loose leaf folder.
- a notebook kept specifically for the course unit you are studying.
- index cards kept in an index box – this will probably only be useful for brief notes, but you could develop a reference system or quotation collection in this way.
- your computer. There is no reason why you cannot take notes straight into the computer. They can then be stored on disk, or printed out on A4 paper and filed.

Developing a filing system

The type of filing system you choose to use relates closely to the method you use for writing notes. A person using A4 paper might choose to file in a different way from the person who uses notebooks. But unless you develop some consistent approach to filing your notes, it will soon become very difficult to find them when you need them.

There are two main ways of filing notes. Either you can adopt a subject-based approach or the 'alphabetical by author' approach. If your study scheme breaks down easily into clear sections or subjects, then it is probably best to file your notes in the same way.

Colour coding

It is possible to develop your own colour coding system for notes. You can use different colour paper for different sets or types of notes. Or what about coloured sticky tabs to mark pages? You may also wish to use different colour inks to distinguish different types of notes. For example, you could use blue for general use, red for useful quotations, green for notes relevant to an assignment, black for biblical references and so on. (But don't make the whole thing so complicated that you spend ages deciding which colour pen you ought to be using for which sentence!)

Here are four different ways of taking notes on the Drane passage we used in the last chapter. Go back and skim read the excerpt again before you look at them. As you read the notes and my comments on them, try to think about which style of notes works for you. There is no one right way of taking notes and you might like to vary the way you take notes according to the type of material involved and your reason for taking notes.

That's

The re-write method

Drane p.139-141

In this section Drane discussed three main questions about the authenticity of the gospel miracles stories. The first concerns the similarities between the N.T. Miracles and other Hellenistic literature. Some similarity to be expected because both are written in same cultural situation. Similarity does not prove or disprove historicity. The second question concerns the claim by some that legendary stories have often been attached to famous people and that this might account for the miracle stories in the Gospels. Compelling evidence against this is a) the early dating of the gospels and hence the chance for witnesses to correct stories, b) the striking difference in the nature of the stories, c) 'Q' – an early gospel strand portrays Jesus as a miracle worker, d) the meaning attached to the miracles. The third question concerns the temptation story and Jesus' choice there not to perform miracles. No real problem here as Jesus was never primarily a wonder-worker. Jesus not after power but humble service. Miracles are never an end in themselves, they are important for what they teach us about God.

This type of note-taking amounts to a rewording of the main points in extended sentences. The advantage is that you have rethought the ideas in your own words. The disadvantage is length.

The linear method

Drane p139-141

3 main questions re authenticity of the miracles:

1. Similarity between gos. m. and Hellenistic parallels
• not surprising due to same cultural situation
• does not mean N.T. not historical

2. The adding on of legendary material to a famous person
• often happens e.g. apocryphal gos. but:
• early date of gos. means stories could be checked
• striking differences in stories
• 'Q' a very early gos. strand also sees J doing miracles

3. The problem of the temptation story and J's rejection of the use of m.
• no great problem here J. only rejects the use of m. for power.

M. never an end in themselves always for what they teach us about God.

This is a very common way of making notes and it has a certain logic to it. The important thing here is to make sure that any abbreviations used can easily be understood when you have to refer back to the notes. Notice the reference to the book and page number at the beginning of the notes. This is important for filing.

my style

Note-taking slows down reading and it won't always be necessary. Don't forget that studying should be enjoyable and if you find a book really interesting and the new ideas stimulating and you are drawn to read on and on, then don't destroy the pleasure by feeling that you must always take notes on every occasion. Notes are for you and to help you. If they help you to get things clear in your own mind then fine, but don't let them become the equivalent to the washing up after the good meal!

Mind-mapping

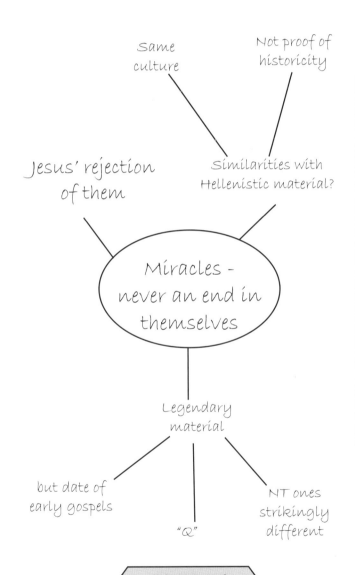

Same culture

Not proof of historicity

Jesus' rejection of them

Similarities with Hellenistic material?

Miracles - never an end in themselves

Legendary material

but date of early gospels

"Q"

NT ones strikingly different

This type of note-taking is very brief but the visual impact can be very helpful to some and can aid memory, especially with added colour or pictures.

Highlighting

spite of the miracles done in them (Mt 11:20-24; Lk 10:13-15).

Perhaps the strongest reason for distinguishing the Gospel miracles from both pagan and later Christian stories is the fact that in the New Testament the miracles mean something. They are not just demonstrations of the supernatural for its own sake. Rather they are an essential part of Jesus' message about the arrival of God's new society.

• There is, however, yet another aspect. It is often pointed out by sceptics that in at least two of his temptations Jesus decisively rejected the temptation to per form miracles (Mt 4:1-11; Lk 4:1-13). He was tempted to turn stones into bread and throw himself from the temple without injury, and he refused to do either. Is it then likely that he would perform in the course of his ministry such a miracle as the feeding of the 5000, which apparently resulted in the crowd trying to make him their king? See Jn 6:1-15; Mt 14:13-21; Mk 6:30-44; Lk 9:10-17).

Only do this with your own books! Use a highlighter, underlining or comments in the margin. The disadvantage with this method is that it discourages you from expressing ideas in your own words and makes it quite difficult to read the original argument of the book straight through ever again. This method can also hinder fresh insights when reading the text for a second time.

A learning journal

A learning journal is a separate note book which you keep for recording your thoughts and feelings about your studies. It doesn't have to be like a dairy where you have a page for every day, but to make it worthwhile I would say that you need to write in it at least once a week. It is a good way of reviewing the work you have accomplished and planning ahead for where you go next.

A journal acts as evidence of all the work you are doing. It will be useful later to look back and see what you have accomplished and how some things have become a lot clearer over time. You could also use a journal to:

- reflect on the implications of some study on an aspect of your Christian life.
- record areas where you have found the work difficult or challenging in another way.
- record a question you want to bring to your study group or your tutor.
- record a question you want to follow up later.
- write down a confusion you feel you have or something you don't understand.
- reflect on the comments made by your tutor about a certain assignment.
- reflect on what you are learning about yourself as a person – the new abilities and confidences you have.
- record mistakes you have made and how you are going to learn from them.

A journal is a form of note taking where you do not distance yourself from the subject in question. It will not help you a great deal with the nitty gritty of a subject but it will help you to relate what you are learning to the person you are   and will enable you to reflect on your growth as a person as you proceed through the course.

Monday: The reading seemed like really hard work. But I did it! There were a few things I didn't understand. Next session must start to write a letter to my tutor about these.

Thursday: This section is making me think through a lot of the things I believed about miracles. How does this relate to God healing people today?

Saturday: A brill session. Got loads done. Really pleased with the assignment. Writing such a full plan seemed to help a lot.

How do you feel about starting a learning journal? What would you write in it about yourself after completing this chapter of this book?

The dreaded assignment

This chapter will help you think about the anxiety you may have about writing assignments and how you can overcome it. It will also help you to think about the possible ways in which you might approach the task of writing an essay or another type of assignment, and the best way of learning from you tutor's comments.

Contents

Assignophobia

-the deep-seated aversion to writing down our best thoughts and insights to be scrutinised by an outside authority

For many people, one of the comforting things about doing a distance learning course is being able to learn and to think on your own. You can develop your thoughts, come to conclusions, change the conclusions later if you want to – all without the fear of someone else suggesting you've got it wrong. For people who are used to 'getting it wrong' in education, this can be wonderfully liberating.

Until they are asked to do an assignment. And suddenly they seize up. It's not that they can't write the assignment. They suffer from assignophobia.

For some students the prospect of sitting down to write an assignment, sending it off and then getting feedback from their tutor is exciting, challenging and extremely satisfying. But for many adults the thought of this is terrifying.

There are a number of good reasons why writing an assignment is a stressful experience for some, and an understanding of these may help to dispel the anxiety:

What it felt like...

...to prepare and send a first assignment

I read the question and thought, 'I can't do this.'

Fearful that I just wouldn't be good enough.

I wasn't sure how to set my work out.

Unsure what standard was expected of me.

I wanted to 'shine'.

I was ready for the challenge, but slightly apprehensive.

I was glad to be getting down to something that would be marked.

Even holding a degree, I was apprehensive that I might after all have missed the point.

I was quite surprised at how much I could do bit by bit.

Writing is personal

Since your first day at school, people have probably emphasised the importance of being able to write well. It is something we all want to be able to do. No one wants to reveal the fact that they find it difficult to express themselves in this way, especially when the ability to write clearly is often associated with an assessment of their intelligence.

But although the ability to write clearly is an important communication skill, it is not an accurate measure of intelligence. There are plenty of people with higher degrees in science subjects who would pale at the thought of writing an essay.

Writing is a personal thing. It is about revealing part of ourselves to another person. It is understandable that we should feel anxious about writing an assignment and sending it off to a total stranger. Your tutor will understand this feeling too. Many tutors will have had to send their own work to other people to mark. And even if they are used to writing, the feeling never entirely goes away.

Writing is decisive

There is something final about writing an assignment. No matter how many books you read and how many notes you take, you finally have to put something down on paper. You have to commit yourself to an idea or an answer.

Committing yourself like that is hard. It means that you have to reject other ways of answering the assignment. It means making up your mind. It also means risking being wrong. No wonder some people try to avoid this commitment for as long as possible and work very close to any deadlines they have.

What it felt like...

...to get a first assignment back from a tutor

Pleasantly surprised, and affirmed.

I was excited at getting a reasonable mark.

I felt reassured that I now had a framework, a standard to aim for.

Initially disappointed with the mark but also encouraged by the tutor's comments.

I wanted to see what I had done wrong.

Don't judge yourself too harshly

No one likes reading what they have written. It never sounds like you think it should. But before you throw it in the bin and start again, think about whose standards you are judging yourself by.

It is very hard these days to escape the written word. It is all around us. But who is it written by? It is written by people who have been selected because they can write.

The articles we read in newspapers and magazines are not the first piece of serious writing the writers have ever done. They will have spent a long time learning and practising their writing skills.

It is wrong to judge yourself by their standards. Everyone has to start somewhere and you may be starting where they started too – at the beginning.

Why assignments?

Most distance learning courses will require you to do some assignments which you send to your tutor for comment and marking. The assignments will mostly take the form of essays but there may also be opportunities for you to do a project or conduct a survey and write a report. On some courses you may be asked to set your own assignment questions or tasks.

But if assignments cause students a great deal of anxiety, why is it that courses insist you complete them at regular intervals?

Perhaps you have memories of writing essays at school or for exams. Did it seem as if the only reason the teacher set the question was to show how little you knew?

On an adult learning course, assignments are not set to show how little you have learnt, but rather how much you know.

Understanding the reasons for an assignment takes away some of the anxiety away about having to write it. Assignments can be set for any of the following reasons:

To help you think

Writing an assignment will deepen your learning. Assignments will usually be set on subjects you have covered in your course note,s and they give you the opportunity to pull your thoughts together. Occasionally they may be set on a different subject which links in with what you have been studying. This means that you have an opportunity to do some independent research.

Students often say that the parts of the course they remember best are the ones they did assignments on. Writing something down for someone else to read means that you have to get your thoughts straight. It means that you have to read around. It sends you deeper into a subject.

To assess your progress

Assignments help both you and your tutor to assess your progress. When you get an assignment back from your tutor, you know how you are doing. The responses given by the tutor will help you to know how you are getting on and point you onwards in ways which develop your thinking further.

Assignments also help tutors do their job. Unless a tutor sees your work, it is very difficult for them to support you and help you with your individual needs. Tutors are there to help you develop your thinking and make you feel at home with the material you are studying. They can only do this if they have something to go on.

To help you develop your powers of self expression

Read through the strip cartoon on this page (yes, you've read it already, haven't you!)

Now imagine you were unable to go out and that you have to write a note to the shop assistant so that a neighbour can pick up the same items for you. The assistant would only have your written words to go on. There would be no help from gestures, pauses and so on. Think about how short the list would be in comparison to the live conversation, and how precise you would have to be.

There are big differences between saying something to someone and writing it down. When two people are talking, they have more than just the words to help them work out what they mean. These extra clues are absent in the written word. You have to be precise and to the point. You have to be able to organise your thoughts in a clear way, and present an argument in a logical fashion.

WHAT TUTORS LOOK FOR

Extension Studies tutors are asked to look out for five features when marking assignments. These are that the student shows:

- an understanding of the content of the study unit
- an ability to address the question as set
- an awareness of a variety of points of view
- an emerging critical faculty
- an ability to interrelate material.

These skills come with time. You will find that as you read the text books you will begin to 'soak up' this way of writing and with time it will become much easier. If you take note of your tutor's comments on the way you presented an assignment and apply them when you write the next, you will find that with each assignment the writing becomes that bit easier.

The keys to success

Have you ever had the annoying experience of going into a shop and being served by a salesperson who clearly doesn't know much about what they are selling? You ask about the product's design or reliability and the salesperson replies with details about when it can be delivered!

A similar problem often occurs when students begin to write essays. One of the most common 'faults' is that students do not answer the question. They latch on to one key word in the question, then merrily write down everything they can find about the topic.

Answer the question

1

The first stage of all successful assignment writing is to decide what the question is asking you to do. Is it asking for a detailed argument or a brief description? Is it asking for a consideration of a topic from a Biblical perspective or from the perspective of one particular Biblical text? As you analyse the question you will get a clearer idea of what the question is. You can analyse a question by looking for the key subjects and key verbs.

Key ideas

In order to write a successful assignment you need to establish what you are being asked to write about. After all, it is no good writing about the way the miracles are portrayed in Luke's Gospel, if the question asked you about the way the miracles are portrayed in the Gospels overall. Looking for key subject words or ideas in the question will help you to establish the exact subject you have to write about.

Underline the key subjects or ideas in questions 1 and 2 on the opposite page. Check your answers with mine on p71.

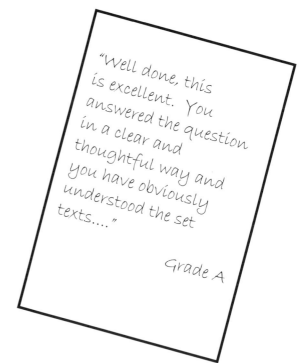

"Well done, this is excellent. You answered the question in a clear and thoughtful way and you have obviously understood the set texts...."

Grade A

Why did this person get such a good mark for their essay? Can you find three reasons in the general comments made by the tutor?

-
-
-

If you don't answer the question your tutor has to assume that you can't.

Key verbs

Once you have established the subject matter of your assignment, you need to know what you are expected to do with it. For example, it is no good retelling the story of the Good Samaritan, if in fact the question asked you to rewrite it in an up-to-date way.

To establish how you have to work with the subject, you need to look for key verbs in the question. These are the words that tell you what to do. You will find a glossary of common verbs used in questions on the opposite page. *Underline the key verbs in questions 3, 4 and 5. Again you will find my answers on p71.*

Spotting the key verbs

This glossary of terms is based on one by Roger Lewis in *How to Write Essays* published by the National Extension College.

Compare Look for similarities and differences between; perhaps reach a conclusion about which is preferable.

Contrast Bring out the differences between

Define Make clear the meaning of a word, phrase or idea.

Describe Give a detailed account of.

Discuss Investigate, set out the arguments, weigh the conclusions, examine the implications.

Evaluate Give your judgment on the issue and then back it up by discussion of the reasoning involved.

Examine Look closely into.

Explain Make plain, give reasons for.

Explore Investigate thoroughly and explain possibly using a variety of viewpoints.

Illustrate Show, make plain or clear.

Justify Show good grounds for decisions or conclusions.

Outline Give the main features or general principles of a subject.

State Present in a clear, precise form.

Summarise Give a concise account of the chief points of the argument or matter. Avoid unnecessary detail.

Trace Give an account of the development of a topic.

Key ideas

Q.1. 'Luke's Gospel is a Gentile Gospel.' Discuss.

Q.2. A recent letter in a magazine attacked the moral influence of the Bible. It quoted Lev. 25:44-46, saying that such passages allowed slave traders to justify their awful business. How would you defend the Old Testament against such attacks, and similar attacks on its support of polygamy and divorce, violence etc.

Key verbs

Q.3. Outline the parable of the unforgiving Servant. Consider the impact the story would have had on Jesus' hearers.

Q.4. Compare and contrast the birth stories of Jesus as recorded in Matthew's and Luke's Gospels. What reasons can you give for both the similarities and differences in the two accounts?

Q.5. 'The time is fulfilled, and the kingdom of God has come near' (Mark 1:15). Discuss the possible interpretations of Jesus' teaching about the kingdom of God.

 ## Now turn over for the other two keys.

Use the course material

2

In most distance learning courses you will find that an assignment clearly follows on from your previous area of study. This is deliberate, as it will help you to deepen your learning. It also means that you will have to go back through your previous work and therefore make your learning that bit more effective. You may also be given specific passages from set books to help you prepare for the assignment. No one is expecting you, especially in the early stages of studying, to write something 'off the top of your head'.

All this means that your tutor will expect to see clear evidence in your assignment of your use of course material. Your tutor will have a clear idea of the texts you have been reading and know the ways in which they could be brought to bear on the assignment.

Using the course material and set texts does not mean that you have to agree with them all. Indeed it is important that your assignment shows an awareness of a variety of points of view. It can happen that, having read the course material on a subject, a student retreats to safe ground, only offering their own views on the subject and being fairly dismissive of others. If the assignment requires it, however, you must not only state the other views, but evaluate them.

Incidentally, no tutor should be interested in making you their disciple. Even if the course material or the tutor prefers a particular view, that does not mean that you have to accept it. Where a tutor is quite justified in being critical is when you make bold assertions without evidence; and your tutor is certainly entitled to show you that there are other ways of looking at issues, if you appear to be ignoring them.

> How might an essay on a Gospel passage differ from a sermon on it? What are the essential features of each? What do you think?
>
> Essay
>
>
> Sermon

Make your points

3

A young child doing a jigsaw may have all the right pieces but that does not mean that she can put them together.

Doing a jigsaw is about identifying the key pieces (corners, outside pieces, distinctive parts of the picture), and then completing the rest of the jigsaw around them. In writing an assignment there is a world of difference between making the important points and mentioning them, almost in passing. Learn to identify the key points and structure your assignment around them.

When you complete a jigsaw, you are constantly looking for linking patches of colour and pattern. The same is true when writing an assignment. Ordering is an essential element in a good assignment. This means that the assignment must have a clear beginning, middle and end, and that you keep the thread of meaning running throughout. You need to make sure that one idea flows smoothly into the next. I will say more about this in the section on 'Tricks of the Trade' on page 70.

Your personal organiser

Assuming that you have examined the question title carefully and have worked out what the key ideas are and what you are expected to do with then, what do you do next? There are five steps in organising an essay, outlined here and the next 2 pages...

1. Collect the information

You are not likely to be asked to write an essay on something you know absolutely nothing about. So the information you require for the essay divides into two types:

Things you already know

The best way of dealing with this is to do a 'brainstorming' exercise. 'Brainstorming' means quickly jotting down the information that immediately comes to mind when you hear or read something, in this case after reading through the essay question. This should take you no more than ten minutes.

You don't need to write in sentences. Just use rough headings. Don't worry if some of the things that come to mind seem wildly irrelevant. Write them down, they may be important. You can choose whether to discard or 'run with' the ideas later. Brainstorming will help you to think 'around' the question.

To gain most help from these pages you must have already read the previous pages on the keys to success

Things you need to know

When you have done this, read through the list again. Ask yourself what you still need to know in order to answer the question.

At this stage, all you can do is write down any questions which you will need to answer in order to be able to write the essay. There may be a key idea in the title which you will have to define in more detail. The essay question may ask for specific information which you are not able to give at the moment. You might want to ask questions about some of the headings you wrote down in the brainstorming session.

These initial steps need not take any longer than half an hour but they will be very useful in guiding your reading. It will stop you plunging straight in and wasting time reading and taking notes on information that you will not need.

When you have done this you can then decide where you will have to look to find the information. You may find that the course writer gives you guidance about what to read. If not, you will have to decide for yourself, using the scanning and skimming skills we looked at in the chapter on reading.

At this stage it is important to take notes on what you decide to read. Make sure that you reference your notes with author, book and page number so that you know where to refer to later on. It is also worth noting down any apt quotations on the subject which you might

2. Make a plan

Once you have completed your reading, you should then make a plan of your essay. Planning helps you to select the important points from the information you have gathered. It helps you to decide which ones you will develop in the course of your essay. Planning also helps you to order the points you will make, thus giving a coherent structure to your essay. Having a plan means that you will have a clear sense of direction when you eventually start to write.

Your plan should consist of a series of headings with one or two ideas under each one. It is important to think about what the logical order is for all the points you wish to include.

Whatever the subject of your essay, it is helpful to think about the plan in three stages:

Introduction: Your opening remarks should set the scene and define any terms used in the question itself; they should state how you intend to tackle the topic.

Main body: This should include all your main points. Before you can write this bit of your plan you will need to go through the notes you made whilst gathering your information and try to group ideas together. If the essay is less than 1000 words, it is probably worth writing down what you plan to write about in each paragraph. If the essay is longer, then you will need to make a list of main points and any sub-points you might wish to include.

It is important to think about the order of your points. If you simply have to make a list of points, then it is usual to put the one you have most to say about first and then work down in order of importance. If, on the other hand, you are putting forward a case or arguing a point, it is important that each point you make is built on the preceding one. This means that you should try to work out an order which will enable you to arrive at the conclusion you would like to draw.

Conclusion: This is often the hardest paragraph to write. It certainly needs careful attention. It may include your final point and may also recall the issues you raised earlier. It may also need to include a brief discussion of the implications of your conclusions. It must, in some way, sum up all that you have said.

If you are using a computer, you will find that steps 3, 4 and 5 blend together. It's worth printing out a draft copy, since it's often easier to spot mistakes on paper than onscreen.

3. Write a draft

With practice you may be able to go straight into writing your essay, once you have a detailed plan and know in detail what each paragraph will contain. But if you are new to essay-writing it is probably worth doing a draft. The disadvantages of doing a draft are that it takes more time and you can find yourself pursuing an ideal unattainable standard in essay-writing proficiency. So weigh it up.

4. Review the draft

Here are some of the questions you should be asking yourself as you read through your draft:

? Are the paragraphs in a logical order?

? Are there any unsupported statements or ideas?

? Is there any waffle? Is all the material necessary?

? Are there any unacknowledged references?

? Have I answered the question? Have I included all the key ideas and followed all the instructions carefully?

? Is the style suitable?

? Does the grammar get 'lost' anywhere (e.g. incomplete sentences)?

5. Write the essay

Go for it! Your tutor will understand how difficult it has been for you to write the assignment and then send it off to them. It will get easier as time goes on and you develop a closer relationship with your tutor.

Thinking ahead

A good essay is not written overnight (although this happens more than it should in a student's life!). It takes time to prepare for an essay and it helps if you take time to reflect on the subject matter before committing yourself to paper. Try planning out in advance how and when you are going to tackle each stage of the process.

If you have a deadline to work to, you may well have to start the process several weeks (or study sessions) before you actually intend to sit down and write it.

If you don't have a deadline it may help if you give yourself one!

Your timetable might look a bit like the one on the right.

By April 15
Do the reading and research

April 19
Write the plan

April 22 and 24
Initial draft and review

April 26
Write it and post it!

Tricks of the trade

In the 'good old days' when people served apprenticeships, they picked up 'tricks' from the craftsmen who taught them. The apprentices soon learnt ways of getting things done quickly and efficiently. There are similar 'tricks' you can pick up when you begin to write essays. The following advice will not help with the content of your essay, but it will help with the way you present information in your assignment.

For a tutor, reading your essay is a bit like setting out on an unknown journey! A tutor never knows exactly where they are going to be taken or even if they will get anywhere! You can help your tutor on the journey through your essay, by 'signposting' the way.

There are a number of ways to guide your tutor through your essay.

☐ Signpost words

Examples of signpost words and phrases are 'however', 'on the other hand', 'although', 'therefore', and 'similarly'. Notice how all these words can be used to link or contrast ideas. They point the tutor on towards what you are going to say. They may also make links with what has already been said. They help your tutor to follow the logic of your argument.

Look back to the article by Drane on pp30-31. Look at the way he begins each of his paragraphs. How many signpost words and phrases can you find? Make a note of them in the box below. Some of the ones I found are at the top of p77.

☐ Topic sentences

Another good way of guiding your tutor on their journey is to begin each paragraph with a short sentence which introduces the topic you are going to develop in the rest of the paragraph. Look at how Drane uses this technique:

> *It is a well-known fact of history that as time goes on miracles tend to be attached to people who are highly regarded for other reasons. We can see this tendency at work in the legends that have been gathered around the lives of so many of the mediaeval saints....*

Drane's first sentence simply introduces the idea that miracles are often added to the life stories of famous people. The rest of the paragraph discusses this idea in relation to the life of Jesus.

☐ Review sentences

A sentence which sums up the argument of your essay so far or reminds the tutor of the journey-so-far, might begin 'So we have seen that...' or 'To summarise...'. This technique, if used occasionally, can be very useful in assuring your tutor that you know what you have been saying!

Presentation

Here are a few golden rules for presenting your assignment:

• Use A4 paper.

• Only write on one side of the paper.

• Leave a wide margin, for your tutor's comments.

• Number the pages.

• Double space the lines for easier marking.

• At the beginning put the title of the essay, your name, and the date of presentation. For longer assignments this could be a separate title page.

• Keep a back-up copy of your essay in case the original gets lost in the post or eaten by the dog!

• Include a bibliography at the end of your assignment.

Preparing a bibliography

At the end of your essay you should include a list of all the books you have used to prepare for the assignment. You should include:

• author's surname and initials

• title (underline or italics)

• publisher, publication date of the edition you used.

For example:

Drane, J, *Introducing the New Testament*, Lion Publishing 1999

My answers
to the exercise on pp64/65

Key ideas

Q.1.   'Luke's Gospel is a Gentile Gospel.' Discuss.

Q.2.   A recent letter in a magazine attacked the moral influence of the Bible. It quoted Lev. 25:44-46, saying that such passages allowed slave traders to justify their awful business. How would you defend the Old Testament against such attacks, and similar attacks on its support of polygamy and divorce, violence etc.?

Key verbs

Q.3.   Outline the parable of the unforgiving Servant. Consider the impact the story would have had on Jesus' hearers.

Q.4.   Compare and contrast the birth stories of Jesus as recorded in Matthew's and Luke's Gospels. What reasons can you give for both the similarities and differences in the two accounts?

Q.5.   'The time is fulfilled, and the kingdom of God has come near' (Mark 1:15). Discuss the possible interpretations of Jesus' teaching about the kingdom of God.

Using quotations

Much of the writing advice on these pages is taken from the St John's College student handbook.

" It is often useful to include quotations in your essays. These may come from text-books, commentaries, articles and from the Bible. Only use quotations to strengthen or illustrate the point you are making. A quotation must serve you and be interpreted by you in the comments which follow. Quotations can also be used to introduce a new point of view and to sum up the arguments so far.

Here are some rules to follow as you think about using quotations:

• Never use them as if they are your own words. Some essays get very near to being transcripts of the course materials and the textbooks! This is called 'plagiarism', and is a serious academic offence. If you are using someone else's words, you must put them in quotation marks and say where you are quoting from.

• Choose shorter rather than longer quotations; they are much more effective.

• Don't substitute quotations for explanation. Your tutor will doubt whether you have really understood the quotation if you leave it unexplained.

• Always give details of your source. Within the text of your assignment it is sufficient to say 'X says', or 'According to P', or 'A believes that' or 'B observes'. At the end of the quotation put the page number of the book in brackets together with the author's name, if you haven't already mentioned it. Alternatively use a footnote to indicate the author's surname and page number of the reference.

• Include full details of the book in your bibliography.

• As a general rule do not write out Bible quotations; it is sufficient to give the reference. It is probably clearest to use colons to distinguish chapter and verses and to use hyphens to indicate passages of scripture. eg. Rom. 1:18 and Rom. 2:1 – 3:8. A useful device is 'ff' which means 'and the following verses'. This allows you to indicate a passage of scripture by where it starts, leaving the ending point vague eg. Rom. 4:1ff. If your essay is concentrating on one particular book of the Bible, it is not necessary to include the name of the book in each reference. The chapter and verse numbers are sufficient.

• If you are using a short quotation of 20-30 words you should keep it within the paragraphing of your text. E.g. Amillennialism, which in the opinion of Dr. Bruce Milne is 'arguably the best interpretation of the biblical teaching on the millennium', does not take a literal view… If you are using a longer quotation then it is best to present it in the form of a separate indented paragraph.

That don't sound right!

We all want to write well, but to do so we need a basic grasp of grammar. For some people the word 'grammar' reminds them of hours spent at school laboriously learning technical terms and structures. Others can't remember ever being taught it at school at all.

Most people can write well without spending hours in formal instruction. Even if your grasp of grammar is poor, you will pick up a lot of the rules almost by accident as you read more. The more you read, the better your grasp of the rules will become. Here are a few simple ways to get started:

Write in sentences

A sentence begins with a capital letter and ends with a full stop. It must have a verb (a 'doing word') and it almost always needs a subject (the person or thing which is 'doing' the verb). Most people can tell if a sentence is right simply by reading it aloud. Read the following. Tick if they sound 'correct':

> Jesus wept.

> Ignatius, Bishop of Antioch, on his way under guard to martyrdom at Rome in about 110 A.D., and meeting many delegations who had come from various Christian communities.

> In the earlier Old Testament books, people are often credited with amazingly long life spans, regularly running into hundreds of years.

> The Gentile church who under the guidance of the Holy Spirit sent two friends.

Now have a go at altering the others so that they become full sentences. (My answers on page 73.)

So check your own grammar by reading your work aloud. You will often be able to tell if there is something missing or if the sentence has become too complicated. Two other tips. Try to vary the length of your sentences. It is very effective to have occasional short, pithy sentences. And try not to begin sentences with weak linking words such as 'and' or 'also' or 'or' (the way I've just done…).

Singular	Plural
criterion	criteria
medium	media
phenomenon	phenomena
stratum	strata

Punctuation.....

...is the way in which the writer gives clues to the reader about how the grammar in the sentence is supposed to work. The most common forms of punctuation are:

• full stop (.) – only for the end of a sentence.
• comma (,) – to indicate you need to take a 'mental breath'.
• semi-colon (;)– best avoided unless you understand its rather complex usage
• colon (:) – best used only to introduce a list.

One of the best ways of learning how to use punctuation and grammar is to look at the way they are used in your set texts. The more you read, the easier all this will become.

C-Nouns	S-Verbs
this advice	to advise
this licence	to license
this prophecy	to prophesy
this practice	to practise

Apostrophes

Most words indicating possession have an apostrophe. Generally, put the apostrophe before the final 's' if the word is singular, and after the final 's' if the word is plural.

> My friend's house = the house belonging to my (one) friend
> My friends' house = the house belonging to my (several) friends

But possessive pronouns (yours, his, hers, its, ours, yours, theirs, whose) do <u>not</u> have an apostrophe. Be particularly careful about "its":

> Its = belonging to it ("Ah my Greek grammar book! I love its thoroughness!")
> It's = it is ("It's raining" where the apostrophe marks a missed letter)

Some names which end with an 's' (eg Jesus, Moses) can show possession simply by adding a final apostrophe: "Jesus' disciples left."

Avoid the temptation to use an apostrophe before the 's' in plurals: "Afternoon teas are served here" (NOT "Afternoon tea's are served here")

Don't copy the example below!

---

all right (two words)

altar (don't 'alter' the place of sacrifice)

anoint (watch out for the multiplying 'n's; an ointment is good for you)

argument (only one 'e')

commitment

complement (complement makes complete; compliment says something nice)

definite (two 'i's)

dependent (when someone is dependent on you they are a dependant)

eschatology (think two 'o's; but only one 'a'ge to come)

existence (no 'tan' in usual British existence)

Galatians (people of Galatia)

There are many **gods** but only one **God**

immediately

indulgences

Isaiah (Is ai ah)

Israel (Is ra el)

Judea or **Judaea**

led is the past tense of 'to lead'. 'Lead' pronounced 'led' is the stuff in pencils.

to loose means to loosen (make less tight); **to lose** is to misplace.

mediaeval

necessary (recess is necessary)

occasionally (the opposite of necessary)

Pharaoh ('Oh' what a pharaoh!)

publicly (be wary of an 'ally' in public)

receive (a piece of advice: don't be deceived; i before e except after c)

The 30 most commonly misspelt words in theological essays

resurrection (re-sur-rection) (Book of; there may be many sights, but the whole is one revelation [singular])

sacrament (Don't think 'sacred' in this case!)

separate (keep on a 'par')

Yahweh (the consonants are more important than the vowels)

Gendered language

Gendered language typically uses masculine forms (such as 'man', 'he', 'his') to include both men and women. It is increasingly the norm in our society to avoid this usage, as a contribution towards ensuring greater equality between men and women. Like any change in the way we speak or write, learning to write 'inclusively' can be tricky at first, but it soon comes quite naturally.

'Man' is not actually that difficult. In a more formal writing style, 'humanity' or 'the human race' sometimes works well, although later in the sentence/paragraph when you want a pronoun, it has to be 'it' (rather than 'he'), which can sound rather impersonal. In a lot of contexts 'people' is a good expression, putting the grammar into the plural and making the pronoun 'they'; and it can actually make the whole sentence feel more personal that the original 'man'.

eg *Man is a fallen creature, and he needs to be redeemed by Christ* becomes:
The human race is fallen, and it needs to be redeemed by Christ.
Or
People are fallen creatures, and they need to be redeemed by Christ.

'He' (meaning he/she or someone) is more of a headache. Talking about 'one' is rather formal and a bit cumbersome. Expressions such as 'he/she' and 's/he' are obviously contrived. 'He or she', 'his or her' can work if used sparingly, and can be effective when you do want explicitly to be inclusive – that is, you want to make the point that what is being talked about is true both of women and of men.

eg. *One is a fallen creature, and one has to be redeemed by Christ.*
Or: *Every person is a fallen creature, and he or she needs to be redeemed by Christ.*

But better than either of these is again to use the plural even when technically you shouldn't. Although many grammarians don't like this, it has a literary pedigree; the use of 'he' to include 'she' was only formalised in 1850. So: 'God send everyone their heart's desire' (Shakespeare) and 'It's enough to drive anyone out of their senses' (George Bernard Shaw). And it is increasingly common today.

eg. *Everyone is a fallen creature, and they need to be redeemed by Christ.*

For more help on inclusive language, see *The Handbook of Non-Sexist Writing for Writers, Editors and Speakers* by Miller and Swift (The Women's Press).

Policy at St John's College

The policy of St John's Extension Studies is to encourage students to use inclusive language in their assignments in an unobtrusive way. This is an encouragement, not a requirement. We recognise that not everyone accepts that inclusive language is a good thing. Students are free to write in gendered language if they wish, including the inclusive use of 'she' which has appeared in some feminist writings. Tutors may comment on the persistent use of gendered language, as part of our encouragement of inclusive expression, but have been instructed that this must not affect the grade given.

Do a project on......

Essays are not the only method of assessment. Increasingly, courses are offering a greater variety of types of assignments. You may be asked to write a project on a certain topic, write a report of an event you attended, or carry out a survey and discuss your findings. You may even be asked to set your own assignment. These types of assignments can often sound more interesting than essay writing, but do not be fooled into thinking that it is easier to get higher marks for this type of work. In fact, you will probably find that you will spend more time completing this type of assignment than you would writing an essay.

Surveys

Beware! Conducting a survey is always much more difficult than you imagine. Most companies employ trained professionals to design questionnaires and carry out research. Working with questionnaires can be problematic for a number of reasons:

• The difficulty of setting a questionnaire that will give you the information you require.
• The need for a large number of people to be surveyed for any meaningful results.
• The problem of analysing the answers given.
• The impact on the results of other factors of which you are not aware.

If you do decide to write a questionnaire, it is probably a good idea to draft one and try it out on a few of your friends. This will help you iron out any misunderstandings people may have about the questions you have asked. Remember that it is much easier to analyse answers where you have stipulated a Yes/No response. It can be very difficult to analyse answers where you have simply left the interviewee to respond in their own words.

Projects

Perhaps you remember doing projects at school. Can you remember how you went about writing a project? Did it involve lots of copying out of books and diagrams and some cutting and pasting of pictures and postcards? If it did, how much of it was really your own work?

To produce a good project takes time and a lot of thought. There are three initial questions that you must answer before you get out the glue bottle and go to town. These are:

Q1.   What is the broad topic going to be?
Q2.   How will you limit the content in order to cover it adequately within the word limit?
Q3.   What do you expect to achieve with this topic within these limits?

Suppose I have a 1000 word limit for my project, and I decided to answer the three questions like this:

A1.   Church buildings.
A2.   A comparison of two church buildings, one Baptist and one Anglican.
A3.   An understanding of how the differing theologies of each Church have affected the design of each building.

Having decided on a topic I would then have to go and research it. Research, in this case, might mean taking time to visit the churches, taking pictures, interviewing the ministers, reading about the history of the buildings and gaining some idea of the fundamental beliefs and practices of both Churches.

One of the ways in which a project can differ from an essay is in the use of pictures, diagrams and graphs. In my project I might include (actual/digital/scanned) pictures of the dedications of buildings, photos I had taken myself, diagrams of the layout of the buildings and perhaps some graphs showing the attendance figures over a number of years. All this could be used to great effect but only if I explained, labelled and commented on the pictures, diagrams and graphs.

Once I had done all this I would then have to make a plan and proceed to present my project in a well-ordered and logical fashion in the same way as I might write an essay.

Writing a report or personal reflection

You may be asked to write a report of an event you attended or write a personal reflection on an experience you went through and what you learned as a result. This is a lot more difficult to do well than it sounds.

Supposing you have been asked to write a report on a church service you attended. The word limit is 800 words. Just as with the project, it is important to establish the main reasons for writing the report and make some initial decisions about the limits of your report and the conclusions you will be able to draw. You could decide to consider the impact on you of the whole service, or just certain parts of it. You could look at the styles of leadership in the service, the make-up of the congregation, the effect of the building on the dynamics of the service – the possibilities are almost endless.

> Jot down any thoughts you have about how you would approach writing a such a report, on a service you have been to recently.

Answers from the exercise on page 70:

Some of the 'signposting' words and phrases used by Drane are: 'In addition', 'In the first place', 'Then there is', 'It is also', 'There is, however'.

Answers from the exercise on page 73 :

The 1st and 3rd are full sentences. The 2nd sentence could read "Ignatius, Bishop of Antioch, on his way under guard to martyrdom at Rome in about 110AD, met many delegations ...." The 4th sentence needs "Who" taking out of it, and is also incomplete. You have to add something about where the two friends went. "The Gentile church, under the guidance of the Holy Spirit, sent two friends to Cyprus"

When you are writing a report on an event or an experience, the description of that event or experience should make up no more than half the report. It is important that you make clear what you have learnt from the experience, what questions you have from the experience and what you intend to do as a result of the experience. Although this type of assignment may not seem to require a lot of reading, you will certainly need to bring the reading you have already done on the course to bear on what you are writing. You may also find that you need to do further reading to help you analyse your experience and learn from it.

Dissertations

Dissertations are longer pieces of writing (anything from 5,000 - 20,000 words). The advantage of doing a dissertation is that you get a chance to choose a subject that really interests you and study it in some depth.

One of the most difficult parts of doing a dissertation is to decide on a title. Make sure that you discuss any title with your tutor and have read quite widely before confirming the title.

Undertaking a dissertation can be quite daunting, but you will be pleased with the end product!

When the work comes back

Sending the assignment off to your tutor is not the end of the learning process for that particular piece of work. There is more learning to do when you get it back. You will probably be concerned to find out the mark you have been given, but...

...your tutor's comments are far more valuable than the mark you have been given.

General comments

These will be either at the beginning or at the end of the comments. These sum up the tutor's assessment of the content of your work and explain your mark.

Structural comments

These might include comments on the structure of your assignment and the logic of sentences and paragraphs.

Evaluative comments

These might include questions about statements you have made, the strength of your argument and your choice of quotations.

Corrective comments

If your facts are wrong, your tutor will point these out.

Points for further thought

It is unlikely that your assignment will become the authoritative piece of work in a particular area! There is always more to be said and thought. Such points are not necessarily criticisms, especially if you get a good mark.

Success and failure

We all want to succeed. There is something about getting a good mark – it seems to tell us something about ourselves. A good grade affirms us and assures us that all is well.

The trouble is, a good mark doesn't always reflect the real worth of what we have learned in the process of writing the assignment. Sometimes we work really hard, do lots of extra reading, have our minds expanded by the issues, but then get in a muddle in trying to write it all up and get a poor mark. At other times we are in a hurry, do the minimum of work but manage to get all the main points down and are surprised at the reasonable mark we get.

There often seems to be no clear correlation between the value we put on a particular piece of work and the grade we get. Other people's standards seem artificial, and out of line with our gut feeling about the worth of our work. We invest so much of ourselves in our work that anything but success feels painful.

It is right that we put ourselves into our learning but we must also remember that when our work does poorly against a particular set of objective criteria, this is not a judgment on us. (It simply means that we didn't answer the question.) Learning is a pilgrimage in which we learn from our successes and failures and build on them.

If you agree with the comments, it is important to think about how you will now approach the next piece of writing you have to do. If you disagree with your tutor's comments, raise the matter with your tutor. Your tutor will welcome feedback. It shows that you are reading and noting what has been said.

A helping hand

This chapter is all about motivation. Studying from home isn't always easy. There will be high points, but there will also be low times when things are difficult. This chapter will help you to think about how you can get the help you need from your tutor and other support structures. It will also consider how you might be able to work through the low points and keep going until you have completed your course.

Contents

Have a look at this graph. It is a picture of what so often happens to levels of motivation on a course of study.

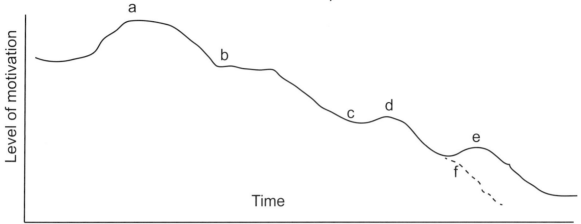

a is the point at which the student applied to do the course.

b is when they actually start the course.

There's a natural decline of motivation between a and b, so the shorter the time between a and b the better. But what happens after b? Motivation frequently continues to fall, whatever the course of study (it's natural, so don't be discouraged!). But within this general decline there are still peaks and troughs:

c is when the the student first heard from their tutor.

d is when the time came for the first assignment to be completed.

e is when the student received their first marked assignment from the tutor.

f is when the student got a low mark.

Motivation levels also depend on a number of other factors :

- Your overall goal
- The type of person you are
- Your level of enjoyment of the course
- How you view success
- The level of support you have.

If you are already studying, stop and think about your own motivation levels so far. What have been the ups and downs for you?

No one feels 100% all the time. You would be an unusual student if you were always filled with enthusiasm! But it is important to be able to manage your feelings towards your work. You will need to build on your enthusiasms and try to avoid sinking into the absolute depths when things aren't going well.

This is where we have to be honest with ourselves. There is no point in hiding the way you feel. Course writers and tutors are aware of the low points that students have. They expect them to happen. They are a common occurrence during any course of study. No one is going to blame you for them.

Admitting that you are not feeling good about the way things are going is the first step in improving the situation. Perhaps you will need to spend a little time reflecting on the effect your feelings are having on you and your approach to the rest of the course. Once you think you have isolated the problem it is important to take some action. This might mean altering your study routine, or seeking help from others, your tutor, other students, or those close to you. Studying should be enjoyable and interesting but there will be times when you will have to work at making it so.

How do you

"I can't cope with this!"

Some parts of any study course are bound to be difficult. Theological concepts and philosophical debates do take some getting into. But if the course made no demands on you, there would be little point in doing it. Perhaps you need to leave this part of the course until another study session when you are less tired. If it is still beyond you, get in touch with your tutor. Your tutor may be able to suggest another approach, or some different reading.

"There's just too much to get through!"

Many students feel like this at the start of a course. There is a lot to get through, but no-one is expecting you to do it overnight! Try to split the course down into manageable units and set yourself a target for completing the first of these. If you feel like this in the middle of a course of study you may need to reassess the way things are going. Have you set unrealistic targets for yourself? Are there other priorities which need your attention for a while? You may need to reassess your target completion dates.

"I'm bored!"

Course writers put a lot of thought into making their courses interesting. One of the golden rules of studying theology is to keep asking, 'What application has this to life – my life, the life of the church, the life of the community or nation or world?' It is possible to study theology in a vacuum without any attempt to apply its lessons to today, but is this really what you want to do? Are you beginning to practise your growing knowledge of the Christian faith in any teaching or preaching you may do and in your own personal reading and devotions?

If the course still seems a bore, then perhaps you do need to ask whether you should be doing it, or whether you are imposing on the course an inner sense of boredom or frustration in other areas of your life.

You and YOUR TUTOR

Most open learning packages provide you with a tutor. You actually buy their professional services when you pay your fees, and it is their job to help you to learn.

Many students feel overwhelmed with awe and dread at the thought of contacting their tutor. Some are overawed by the massive intelligence and knowledge they assume a tutor must have. Others feel dwarfed by the system when they are allocated a tutor who seems to be no more than a faceless name and address.

These reactions are understandable, especially if you left school quite a long time ago. Then, the teacher knew it all and you had to learn it. Perhaps it was obvious from the way the teacher related to you that they didn't really understand you – only their subject. Knowledge was awesome, impenetrable and impersonal. Silly questions from pupils were irritations to the smooth running of the class.
It is hard to make the shift from child education to modern adult education, but it is extremely important you do.

> *Your tutor is your partner in the learning process, and it is a partnership of equals.*

You are equals in every way except for the expertise that your tutor has in the area you are studying.

A relationship...

Adult learning is not impersonal. The more you and your tutor know about each other, the better you will be able to work together.

Here are some of the things that students have said that they would like to know about their tutors. Tick the ones which seem important to you :

... name and how they wish to be addressed

... telephone contact number and availability

... availability for one to one meetings

... qualifications

... interests in the subject area

... previous experience of tutoring

... other jobs, if they are not full-time tutors

... hobbies

... family

... preferences about email

This page is partly based on material from Chapter 8 of Derek Rowntree's book *Teach Yourself with Open Learning*, Kogan Page, 1993

If your study system gives you the chance to meet your tutor you will be able to get most of the information you need in the course of the discussion. If you do not have an opportunity to meet then you may find that your tutor will send you a letter or a personal biography. If your tutor doesn't offer the information you think you need, then you may want to ask for it. Try writing a letter, perhaps including some information about yourself and then suggesting a few things you would like to know about them.

It is equally important for your tutor to know about you and why you are doing the course. Unless you enter into some kind of relationship with your tutor, learning will be limited. What you need to learn from the course may be very different from what someone else needs to learn – because we are all different people. Your tutor may ask for specific details about you. If they don't, you could try writing to them, telling them about your family, Christian background, educational qualifications, why you wish to do the course and any difficulties you think you may encounter.

...of a particular kind

Your tutor isn't like the old fashioned schoolmaster standing over you brandishing the cane, but nor can they be an indulgent parent either. We all like people to tell us how wonderful we are from time to time but this is not generally the role of your tutor!

There are some ways in which the student /tutor relationship is different from any other relationship you may have with adults. Some of the usual conventions of politeness are not there. You will often be told (hopefully in the nicest possible way...) how you measure up to a set of objective standards. This very direct or frank way of commenting on your work may sometimes sound critical or even a little rude. We are

not used to being told exactly the way things are by other adults and often we would prefer it anyway if our friends kept those points of view to themselves. If a tutor is to help you in the learning process, they must be able to comment critically on your work, to tell you when you are not making any sense or where you have clearly not understood the subject matter. It is only as a result of this sort of honesty that you will be able to put the problems right and achieve your full potential as a learner.

> *Your tutor is not judging you. It is rather that some aspect of your work is causing your tutor some concern.*

Tutors are aware of how difficult it can be to receive criticism, and sensitivity is called for on their part. There must be a relationship of trust between you and your tutor. Hopefully you will come to know that your tutor genuinely has your best interests at heart.

Your course notes should explain how long it should take for a tutor to mark and return an assignment to you. You are prefectly within your rights to expect the tutor to abide by these guidelines. If you hear nothing from your tutor, then pursue the matter. Complain if there are unreasonable delays.

Email

Email has transformed distance learning. It is a convenient and cheap way to communicate with your tutor and often quicker than the phone because you do not have to keep leaving messages! Many tutors are willing to receive assignments as email attachments and will mark them this way. Different courses have different regulations and conventions about this so check first and agree on an appropriate file format.

Phone

If you are given a tutor's telephone number this indicates that they are willing to be contacted by phone. This can be a very effective way of getting tutorial advice, especially when you are stuck or confused (when it can be very hard to put your difficulty on paper). Most students use the telephone too little. Don't be shy about phoning if the service is part of your contract, but remember to ask if you are phoning at an inconvenient time and, if so, fix a time to ring back.

Plugging in to what's available

Most providers of distance learning courses realise how important it is that you have contact with other people. They therefore put thought and resources into the 'personal' support you need. But many students do not use these support structures to their full advantage. There may be a number of different resources you can turn to.

Residential schools

Some courses will offer short residential periods as part of your study. Sometimes they are compulsory. Often students are quite fearful of going on these, and feel as if they are about to set off for that first day of school all over again. Going on a 'residential school' will be very different from your own experience of school. You will find that there is an atmosphere where everyone, students and tutors, is learning together.

Spending a week away from home can be an enormous boost to your study. You can stop struggling to find the time to study. You will have time to think at length about things. You will also have the opportunity to meet different tutors who will be able to offer a wide range of knowledge and may help in a way that your own tutor has not been able to.

Meeting with other students and tutors also gives you the opportunity to bounce ideas off each other and sort out what you yourself really believe about difficult issues. Often this kind of reflection doesn't happen until you begin to talk about it with others. In this atmosphere there is the opportunity for you to shed some of the prejudices we all develop through life, or begin to think about something you may have believed for years without asking why you believe it. As you listen to others you will also become aware of other ways of approaching a subject which are as valid as your own.

One of the other benefits of going on a residential school is the opportunity you have to get to know other students. When you are studying at home it is often difficult to feel that you are a 'real' student. You may feel as if your studies are on the edge of your life. Meeting other students redresses the balance. You realise that you are part of a great number of people who share the same interests and concerns as you do. There will be lectures – and the chance to fire questions at the lecturers. There will also be plenty of time for group discussion, both formally and informally. You won't always come up with the answers to all the questions you have, but together you will come to new points of discovery about what the questions are. And when you ask questions, they won't be just your questions, they will be questions that others share.

Many students cite their residential experience as one of the highlights of their study. They go home with new ideas about how to study and a deeper understanding of the subject. Residential schools are an incredible learning resource and if you have an opportunity to go on one, make it a priority.

Feedback

from students who have attended summer schools at St John's, Nottingham

The diverse mix of participants led to lively and fresh discussion.

The structure of lecture-seminar-feedback gave an excellent opportunity to think through the material, work out applications and ask questions.

There was never a feeling of being pressed to accept a particular line of thought or point of view.

The main value of the lectures was compelling me to arrive at my own point of view.

I was able to see how the information I have fits together into the whole, and I began to ask the right questions

I found the meeting with others probably the most rewarding bit of the whole week.

I was extremely sad at leaving, although I think my family were pleased to see me back.

I learned a lot about different methods of Bible study, and incidentally about myself.

Local study groups

Your course may offer facilities for you to join with other students in your area for support meetings. Sometimes this is compulsory. Some courses offer group tutorials within your locality. Other kinds of groups have no tutor input and set their own agenda. It is important that you check out what the group in your study course aims to do and then use it to the best advantage.

Some people get more out of groups than others. This may depend a bit on your personality. But even if you find groups uncomfortable, most of us benefit from sharing our thoughts and feelings with others and listening to theirs. Groups need a regular commitment of time and you need to weigh this up.

If you are interested in setting up your own support group, St. John's Extension Studies produce a booklet on *How to run a mutual support group*.

Former students

Some courses offer you the chance to contact former students who are willing to act as advisors or mentors. Past students will undoubtedly have faced some of the problems or pressures that you are facing and may well be able to offer some good advice.

You may find that a former student can help you:
- to decide which courses will most suit you
- to clarify what you are trying to do in an assignment.

They will do this:
- by talking through any learning problems you may have
- by sharing some of their skills and expertise with you.

These people are often not paid for the help they give you but they have offered their services and will be pleased if you make the most of them.

Are you isolated?

A lot has been said about the isolation of 'distance learning'. The problem of isolation is certainly acute in theoretical or specialised areas of study, like pure maths or molecular biology. Here the only way to engage with other people in your learning is to engage with tutors and other students. It really is 'nose into the books and tell everyone around to go away' – because no-one around is a participant in this particular quest for knowledge.

The same is simply not true for a life science like applied theology. The fact that there is no-one around who is doing your particular course to talk to about God, does not mean that there is no-one around to talk to about God. There are people in churches around you who are also seeking to understand God and the Bible better. They may be pursuing this quest in a very different way from you – and certainly it might be difficult to get them engaged in a detailed discussion of your next assignment! But unlike the pure maths student, you are better off than you would be if you were living in a remote cottage in the Scottish highlands (apologies to you if you are studying in the remote parts of the Scottish highlands..). One of the great benefits for you in distance learning is that you are immersed in the life of a church, and there is great learning potential there.

The successful study of applied theology away from a centre of teaching, depends on being able to maximise your contacts with people and situations around you, to the advantage of your studies. If you can create interaction between you, the material and the church/world around you, you are actually practising the very stuff of theology. Don't fight it!

A question of value

Perhaps some of your non-Christian friends ask you why you bother to do all this work in studying theology for no obvious outcome. After all, you are not likely to get promotion in your job because you have a qualification in theology, nor are you getting any immediate social benefits from doing the course. In fact, they may see it as a hindrance to a better life. So what are the benefits?

Your Christian friends may not be much more sympathetic. When the world desperately needs the basic gospel of the love of God preached and demonstrated by followers of Jesus, why are you sitting around reading books? It's not as if you even appear to be getting any holier! If anything, you seem to be more reflective and 'aloof' from the immediate activities of church life.

A better knowledge of the Christian faith does have practical benefits to the disciple of Jesus. Knowing God and loving our neighbour are closely linked in the Christian faith, and Christian knowledge that is not fruitful in day-to-day Christian living has something deficient about it. But although Christian knowledge does produce practical action, it is not merely a tool for producing action and must not be judged by its utility value.

Rightly studied, theology is of great practical value in Christian discipleship but it does not need to be constantly justified in this way. Like the lover who delights to learn all kinds of apparently insignificant things about the one he or she loves, our desire to know Christ and understand his ways is simply part of our fascination with the most interesting person who ever lived. The riches of Christ do not need to have immediate cash value.

Running out of steam?

Often students find that their motivation levels go down as they get into the course. Occasionally it can feel as if you are coming to a complete halt in your studies. This can be depressing or unnerving. It is useful to think about this before it happens to you.

We all find different things satisfying. Some enjoy gardening, for others it is a chore. Some get real enjoyment from taking part in a sport, others do it purely because it will keep them healthy.

There are two types of satisfaction:

You get intrinsic satisfaction when the task or activity is its own reward. For example, swimming a mile purely because you enjoy swimming, or the enjoyment you get from taking a sip from a cup of tea or from a pint of beer on a summer's afternoon.

You get extrinsic satisfaction from something when there is a valued outcome associated with the activity you are engaged in. For example, swimming because it keeps you fit, gardening because you like to have a pleasant garden to sit in in the summer.

Sometimes the same task is capable of giving either type of satisfaction – and which it gives depends on the sort of person you are.

What activities do you enjoy doing? Write some of them down.

Then try to identify which type of satisfaction you get from each of the activities you listed. You might find that some activities give you both types of satisfaction.

Did you have more intrinsic or more extrinsic satisfactions? The balance between the two types of satisfaction may simply reflect the tasks you chose in answering the question, but it may reflect a general balance in you.

Some people are very good at ignoring long-term goals and can concentrate on tasks that have short-term results. Other people persevere with tasks that have little intrinsic satisfaction in order to bring about a worthwhile long-term goal or reward.

Which type of person are you?

o   I can work towards long term goals

o   I prefer to see immediate rewards

Most students undertake distance learning programmes because of the long term, extrinsic rewards. There may be a qualification to be aimed for, or a specific ministry which you will be able to exercise once the study has been completed. Or you may simply want to deepen your knowledge of God.

If you are the type of person who is motivated by extrinsic rewards, then it is likely that you will find motivation less of a problem. On the other hand, the less long-term rewards motivate you, the more you will have to find ways of enjoying the immediate process of study. It may also mean that you need to try to split up the course into smaller units and treat yourself to a reward every time you complete one (a Mars Bar, watching a film, or whatever).

Working as a team

A personal tutor can be asked to fulfil a number of different roles. Your course material should give you some guidelines about the sort of relationship you can expect to have with your tutor. It is important that you realise the parameters of the relationship you have.

Some courses only expect their tutors to be contacted for reasons directly to do with the material you are studying. Others make tutors available to their students to discuss other study-related issues. Very few courses will employ tutors to help you with more personal matters.

You can however expect your tutor to provide the services you have paid for; and although these may be spelled out in the paperwork of your course, you may need to agree particular details in a conversation or letter to your tutor.

The material on these pages will help you make the most of the help your tutor gives you.

A resource

Despite the advantages there certainly are in studying at home on a distance learning course, there are particular difficulties which you will have to face.

Students taking courses in an educational institution can discuss their courses and the ideas they have for assignments with fellow students. They can share ideas and resources. This is reassuring. When it comes to writing an assignment they help each other to decide on the sort of work to aim for, how long to spend on it and so on.

On a distance learning course, you work alone and do not have this extra help. Your tutor will understand that you will sometimes want to contact them before you begin to write an assignment. You may want clarification of the essay title or some help with resources for the assignment. Your tutor will understand the isolated position you are working from and take this into account in tutoring you.

A troubleshooter

No one waits until a ship is on the verge of sinking before sending out an SOS message. Once you realise you are in serious trouble, you need to shout for help. There is then more time for a rescue operation to be mounted. It is important that if things are going badly, you let your tutor know. You should contact your tutor when:

• you get stuck or get totally confused. Tutors are busy people but they expect you to contact them when you get bogged down and are finding it difficult to proceed. They will want to support you in your studies, and give specific explanations and advice.

• you stop working. If you are prevented from getting the work done because of other commitments, or are consciously taking a break from your studies because of other pressures, let your tutor know so that they don't worry unduly about you! It is not their role to pester you to complete the course. Whether you do the course or not is your decision. But you may get some useful advice.

Regular use of the support structures offered by your tutor will reduce the likelihood of you having to send out an SOS message. It will also help with problems of motivation.

Getting the help you need

There may be occasions when you feel that you are not getting very helpful comments from your tutor. Perhaps they seem too vague or point to weaknesses in your work without telling you how to put things right. If this is the case, you need to make this clear. When you next write to your tutor try saying things like:

'You've said that I am not making the points in a precise manner. Could you highlight where this happens in the essay?'

'You commented that my argument was weak. Could you tell me where the weak points are?'

'You say my essay sounds more like a sermon than a piece of academic work. Could you suggest a couple of ways I might improve my essay-writing style?'

Tutors are human beings and they do sometimes get things wrong. They may not realise how unclear they have been or exactly what you need to know. Be patient with them. They will usually respond to a friendly enquiry!

A two-way conversation

The major task your tutor has is to comment on your written work. They will spend a considerable amount of time writing reflections on it and reactions to it. It is important that you take notice of these. Learning is the pursuit of understanding, but learning breaks down when it stops being an ongoing process, when you stop building on the insights and questions raised by your tutor.

Some of the things you might need to do as a result of your tutor's comments are:

- re-read your work in the light of the comments.
- think about how you could improve this assignment and future ones.
- re-read any sections of the course your tutor draws your attention to.
- check your notes – do they need correcting in the light of incorrect information you may have put in the assignment?

In order to take full advantage of the help your tutor can give you, you must be prepared to become involved in a conversation or dialogue with your tutor over the issues that arise as part of your course. Tutors appreciate it when students 'come back' with further questions and comments. A tutor who writes detailed comments and never gets any reaction from you to these 'learning points' will wonder what effect the comments had, or even whether they were read at all! It is important for your learning, and for your relationship with your tutor, that you take note of tutor comments and pursue them with your tutor as appropriate.

Handling the pressure

Pressure can be a very creative thing and there will be pressure put on you by the internal demands of the course. But too much pressure will have a negative effect on your level of motivation.

Sometimes you really want to get on with our work but external pressures keep you from doing so. Perhaps a relative falls ill, your job becomes more demanding, or you move house, have a baby and so on. Often these pressures are unplanned and really do throw you. They might mean that you stop studying completely for a while. Alternatively, you might be trying to carry on studying through these difficult times but finding that you are not managing to reach the targets you have set yourself. Perhaps it feels as if you can never concentrate on the task in hand. This is bound to affect your overall motivation level.

If you feel like this, try thinking about the following:

• Do you need to take a break from studying?

• Do you need to reorder your priorities? (See the exercises in Chapter 1)

• Is there something you could 'let go' of? Even temporarily…?

• Do you simply have to keep going but recognise that it is not the course itself which is problematic but other external things affecting your attitudes?

Whatever the problem, it is worth letting your tutor know. They may not be able to help directly but will understand if you have to slow down for a while.

Hands up for help

This chapter has concentrated so far on the human resources you have to help you to study. It is right that we finally think about the resources we have in God. As Christians we are not left on our own. Christian truth is not something which we have to work out entirely by rational processes. God gives us His Spirit and reveals His truth to us through the Spirit (John 16:13-15).

Theology has been described as 'thinking God's thoughts after him'. Spending time with God is bound to help! A very important part of study of the Christian faith is our reliance on God to be there and to guide us. This is one helping hand who won't let us down. Studying the Christian faith is no substitute for a life of prayer and an important part of your study programme will be the prayer you surround it with and the dependence you have on God to be there alongside you.

You may like to turn some of the ideas in this chapter into prayer. What would you like a helping hand with at the moment?

Paul's prayer

I pray that, according to the riches of his glory, he may grant that you may be strengthened in your inner being with power through his Spirit, and that Christ may dwell in your hearts through faith, as you are being rooted and grounded in love. I pray that you may have the power to comprehend, with all the saints, what is the breadth and length and height and depth, and to know the love of Christ that surpasses knowledge, so that you may be filled with all the fullness of God (Eph.3:16-19)

A question of faith

In this chapter we look at issues which arise from studying the Christian faith as committed Christians.

Contents

Why study your faith?

You have decided to study your faith. I think you have made a good choice. But do you know why? And can you support your decision?

Why are some Christians keen to be adding all the time to their fund of biblical knowledge and understanding, while others seem content to eke out their Christian existence with whatever titbits of spiritual insight happen to fall from the preacher's lectern? Some Christians love to learn. Others are happy to accept that we will never understand everything about God, and so the fact that we are pretty ignorant is merely relative. Others again resist the idea as endangering a simple trust in God, or as a pointless waste of time when there is so much to do.

Wise enough for tomorrow?

There was a time when Toffler's *Future Shock* was the trendy book to read. His warnings about the long-term effects of the accelerating pace of change in society was certain to get an interesting discussion going. Were things really going to go that way? For those eager and impatient for change anyway, it was all rather exciting…

The effects of rapid change are already with us – even in the church. The most fundamental of those effects is on what we 'know'.

The half-life of an electronics engineer (the time it takes for half of what they know to become obsolete) was recently put at two years. I wonder what the half-life of a Christian is today, in relation (say) to ethical and social issues. Longer than that maybe, but it is getting shorter.

When the shape of the questions keeps on changing, the answers of yesterday no longer fit.

Because of this pace of change, Toffler argued that our society must become a 'learning culture' where everyone expects to learn and to change – and knows how to. We need a learning culture in the church too, where we all see it as part of our normal Christian lives to be constantly thinking out the Christian message in relation to our fast-moving society.

The zealot tendency

Perhaps the greatest danger of 'future shock' is that people come to feel that they can no longer weigh up issues for themselves. They therefore retreat into the certainties of a particular tradition, or they accept the dominating leadership of someone who sounds as if they know where to go.

For a few weeks of 1993, the world watched the drama of Waco and the personal Armageddon of David Koresh and the Branch Davidians. Now they are dead, children among them. David Koresh was able to manipulate others not because he was evil or clever, but because they chose to believe him when he said that he was a better interpreter of scripture than they were. Koresh's followers did not need to trouble themselves with the complexities of the Christian faith, because he would worry for them. They did not see the need to weigh up the issues for themselves.

Theological study involves taking responsibility for our own faith. We reflect on a perspective on God and the world, to which we are personally committed above all else. It is painful to re-examine our interpretations of it – we have invested in it so much of who we are. But if we fail to study at this level, we become trapped in the zealot tendency .

The value of the past

There's no future for the church if we keep our eyes on the good old days of the past. If the future is uncertain, then all that really matters is the present – an up-to-date faith focussed on a contemporary interpretation of the Scriptures. So why spend time on biblical background, church history, historical doctrine?

We often think of the Christian life as a journey, leaving the past behind and pressing boldly on into the future. The trouble with looking forward to the future with our backs to the past is that we just don't see a lot. The future hasn't happened yet.

Someone suggested to me that life is more like rowing a boat up a river. What you see as you 'look forward', what is open to your gaze as far as the eye can see, is where you have just been and the banks on either side of you. You see where you are going by the odd look over your shoulder, using your view back down the river as your frame of reference.

This rang true to me. I commend it not only as an image for life but also as a perspective on your studies. Careful and thoughtful reflection can only be made of the past, because at least you can see it. You achieve a depth of reflection and knowledge not possible in relation even to our fast-changing present, let alone the uncertain future. From

**Then we will no longer be infants, tossed back and forth by the waves, and blown here and there by every wind of teaching...
(Eph. 4:14)**

this depth of understanding comes the ability to interpret and steer into the future, even when our knowledge of the future is restricted to the odd look over our shoulder.

The study of the Christian past, whether in the Scriptures or in church history, is a recognition of the fact that life has to be lived this way – looking forwards into the past and looking backwards to the future.

This is the powerful position to row from – try rowing a boat facing forwards and you'll soon find you make very slow progress! Our confidence for the future rests partly in our knowledge that this boat has already come down a long stretch of water. We will direct its course better by learning the lessons of its journey so far, than by peering into a misty future and hoping to make up the journey as we go along.

Photo by courtesy of www.picture-newsletter.com

Criticising the Bible

Many Christians who begin to read more serious books on theology get a nasty shock. They find things very dear to them being treated as objects of speculation and even disdain. Even the most sacred tenets of Christianity seem to be up for grabs. It can feel like overhearing an unkind conversation about the virtues and vices of one's spouse! Many then reject theological study as destructive of committed faith in Christ.

'Critical study of a book of the Bible destroys my devotional use of that book for months and even years to come.'

(A theological student)

Nowhere is this more true than in the 'critical' study of the Bible. We are simply not used to asking the kinds of questions that biblical scholars ask – and we are certainly not as nonchalant as they appear to be about the answers! For us the Bible has been the channel of God's living word to us. Anything which even appears to question its validity or credibility is easily perceived as sacrilege.

Coming to terms with a more 'detached' study of the biblical documents and marrying this with a clear commitment to biblical truth is a long pilgrimage for most Christians. For you, answers may be slow in coming. As you seek for them, here are themes to look out for.

Diversity

A devotional reading of Scripture tends to see it as a single piece, welded wonderfully together over the centuries by the Holy Spirit. Discovering its diversity can be a disturbing experience.

The Books of Kings just don't see things the same way as the Books of Chronicles. Some prophets seem full of hope and others full of doom, in much the same circumstances. Reconciling the accounts of the four gospels is easier in general than it is in detail. Paul is pretty scathing about 'works' and James doesn't see much virtue in 'faith'.

Where does such diversity stop being an 'enriching paradox' and start becoming an irreconcilable difference?

The diversity of Scripture is hard for any tidy system of Christian belief – not just evangelicalism but all other -isms. As we study, we may need to allow the diversity we find in the Bible to begin to question our attachment to our particular -ism.

Often we can be helped by simply asking what a particular passage of Scripture was for. Was it meant to inspire? To challenge? To inform? To teach or prove doctrine? To be a vehicle of worship? If we use it in line with its original intention, we are less likely to find it in conflict with other parts of Scripture.

Criticism

Did Moses write the Pentateuch? Is the whole book of Isaiah written by one prophet or several? Is Jonah an historical account or a story with a point to make? If Jesus said all the memorable things he is meant to have said in John's gospel, why aren't they recorded in the other three gospels? Did Paul write all the letters which bear his name?

The questions seem endless – and even pointless. Why do scholars keep asking such questions? (I guess because they can make a living doing it...) Are they trying to help me to a more honest and open appreciation of Holy Scripture? Or is it really a humanistic attempt to erode the authority of God's Word?

"A Christian is a person who thinks in believing and believes in thinking"

(St Augustine)

Whatever the motives, we have to come to terms with the questions raised. But we need not answer them all yet. Often we need a wider appreciation of the field of study before we can sensibly decide on our opinions on such things. We can 'put them in the freezer' until we are ready to tackle them.

The greatest virtue in all kinds of education in our modern humanistic world is detached enquiry. The conclusions of anyone who has a vested interest in particular "answers" are always suspect. All previous convictions about the subject under enquiry are considered to be prejudices. For many in higher education, committed Christians who study their faith lack all academic credibility.

Inspiration

All Christians believe that the Bible is inspired in some sense. In fact most biblical scholars do too. But in what sense?

Many 'systems' of Christian belief (-isms again) have insisted that inspiration necessarily implies infallibility. If it is the word of God, it cannot be wrong or mistaken in any detail. This has allowed them to build intricate systems of doctrine supported and 'proved' at every point by an unquestionable authority. Are they right? And who decides whether they are right?

As we study Scripture we may be able to find ways in which the Bible itself defines what it means by 'an inspired word of God'. You might perhaps find a more creative and 'inspiring' answer than many systematic theologians have found.

Boring?

Why do we make the Bible so boring? Thrilling episodes of God's loving activity in this world are read in church like a funeral oration. Has our devotion to the Bible turned the living Word of God into a big black book and made it dull?

As your conventional views of Scripture are questioned, look for the silver lining. Unfamiliar questions may liberate you in your creative use of the Bible in the church, and give it fresh power to *speak* to today's world.

Hermeneutics

Hermeneutics is the system of principles governing the interpretation of language (in particular, literature). What does a passage of Scripture mean? How can we decide between different interpretations? What are the principles upon which such a decision is based? Are the principles involved the same for the Bible as for all other literature?

Theology and the Church need to learn to listen to each other more.

One of the basic principles of hermeneutics is that a passage means what the author intended it to mean. A passage of Shakespeare means what Shakespeare intended to convey in writing it. The task is to judge that as accurately as possible. For many Christians this principle is complicated in relation to Scripture because they see the 'real author' of the Bible as the Holy Spirit. The 'real meaning' is then hard to define.

Closely related to this is the issue of applying the message of Scripture to today. Do the values of the Hebrew culture in which the Bible was largely written also have biblical authority? Is the ancient worldview normative for us (is the earth flat?) – and if not, how far does this go? What, for example, about the place of women?

The Bible is a human book. It is written in human language. It is the message of God 'incarnate'. All human relations are to some extent subjective. Interpreting human language is also to some extent subjective. It is caught as well as taught. It is an ability more than a skill. Hermeneutics is really about developing that ability.

A modern parable

Two people return to their long neglected garden and find among the weeds a few of the old plants surprisingly vigorous. One says to the other, 'It must be that a gardener has been coming and doing something about these plants.'

Upon inquiry they find that no neighbour has ever seen anyone at work in their garden. The first man says to the other, 'He must have worked while people slept.' The other says, 'No, someone would have heard him and besides, anyone who cared about the plants would have kept down these weeds.' The first man says, 'Look at the way these are arranged. There is purpose and a feeling for beauty here. I believe that someone comes, someone invisible to mortal eyes. I believe that the more carefully we look, the more we shall find confirmation of this.'

They examine the garden ever so carefully and sometimes they come on new things suggesting that a gardener comes, and sometimes they come on new things suggesting the contrary and even that a malicious person has been at work. Besides examining the garden carefully they also study what happens to gardens left without attention. Each learns all the other learns about this and about the garden.

Consequently, when after all this, one says 'I still believe a gardener comes' while the other says 'I don't', their different words now reflect no difference as to what they have found in the garden, no difference as to what they would find in the garden if they looked further and no difference about how fast untended gardens fall into disorder.

At this stage, in this context, the gardener hypothesis has ceased to be experimental. The difference between one who accepts and one who rejects it is now not a matter of the one expecting something the other does not expect. What is the difference between them? The one says 'A gardener comes unseen and unheard. He is manifested only in his works with which we are all familiar.' The other says, 'There is no gardener.'

The one calls the garden by one name and feels one way about it, while the other calls it by another name and feels in another way about it. And if this is what the difference has become, then is it any longer appropriate to ask which is right or which is reasonable?

'A Modern Parable' is taken from the article 'Gods' by J. Wisdom in Proceedings of the Aristotelian Society 1944-45

The value of doubt

"Doubt is not the opposite of faith, unbelief is. Doubt does not necessarily or automatically mean the end of faith, for doubt is faith in two minds. What destroys faith is the disobedience that hardens into unbelief"
Os Guinness

Detached intellectual enquiry is the great virtue of modern higher education. You have to allow yourself to doubt things you have always held to be true if you are going to learn properly. Certainty about these beliefs in the face of evidence to the contrary shows an unwillingness to learn. This is true in theology as much as in other disciplines.

The trouble is, this goes against the grain of what we have learned in the church. We are taught that the truth of the gospel makes no sense to the unbeliever. So if the beliefs of the Christian faith are criticised by intellectuals as being irrational, or even just open to some debate, this is of no great significance. If we listen to them, if we allow ourselves to doubt, we may find ourselves on the path to unbelief.

Theology and the Church are often in conflict over doubt. Theology sees it as necessary and healthy; the Church often sees it as destructive of faith. For both it is a life and death issue, gnawing at the heart of what each believes and stands for. So there is often little toleration of each other over doubt.

• The Church tends to see theology as an ivory-tower exercise. Some clergy disdain their theological training from the pulpit. We are encouraged not to be sidetracked from the path of faith by the empty debates of theology.

• Theology tends to see Christianity as an interesting object of historical interest. Theology has become the study of what people believed. It does not see itself as a commentator on an ongoing reality, continually shaped by God's current activity in the Church and the world.

And in our study of theology, we must allow the 'disciple' side and the 'student' side of our Christian lives to be in constant conversation. That means that as disciples we must learn to handle doubt, and as students we must learn to handle certainty. This will become an essential part of our Christian pilgrimage.

Faith is not certainty

The 'doubting bishops' controversy in the 1990s has highlighted the importance of the objectivity of Christian truth and the appropriateness of church leaders actually believing it. Yet those issues must not blind us to the fact that doubt is an essential part of the pilgrimage of Christian knowledge. We must weigh up theological issues, without pre-judging what the answers 'must' be because of our traditions.

Doubt is the terrain over which faith must pass towards certainty. We must allow ourselves to doubt in order to reach a new point of certainty. Passing through the terrain of doubt is part of the journey of faith. Theological study is not about tapping into prepackaged certainty to build you up in the faith. It is designed to give you practice in passing through the terrain of doubt and finding new and surer points of certainty.

Of course there is also the journey of doubt, where people explore the terrain of doubt as an end in itself and resist arriving at any point of certainty even when it is staring them in the face. Certainty is not very trendy in some theological circles, and the pressures on theologians (and theological students) to resist certainty is considerable. Doubt can be a comfortable cul-de-sac rather than an uncertainty to be traversed.

But doubt is an inevitable ingredient in the journey of faith. It digs deeper foundations for certainty than certainty can itself. Faith is exploring doubt, seeking certainty. It is not certainty of mind itself.

Theology and spirituality

'Theology implies participation in a religious faith, so that some experience of the life of faith precedes theology. ... The process of bringing the content of the faith-experience to clear expression in words embarks us on the business of theology.'

John Macquarrie, Principles of Christian Theology SCM 1966

Christian young people are sometimes warned against going to University to study theology, in case they lose their faith. And it does happen. Away from the reassurance of unquestionable certainty from the pulpit, and in the midst of the sceptical questioning of some modern theology, young Christians can find that their faith did not have deep enough roots.

All our learning about the Christian faith runs two risks:

Too dry

Theology has gained a reputation for being dry. Too many books on theology seem arid and dusty, merely an intellectual exercise which does not provide the kind of ground in which the plant of faith can grow. We can sometimes feel that the pages of a textbook will flake and crack with the dry theoretical arguments and obscure information found on them. We then ask, 'What good is this doing my faith?'

Too wet

But equally dangerous for any plant is the kind of ground that is awash, without proper drainage. Slushy Christianity kills off faith just as much as dry theology does. 'Lay down my mind and will' can be an act of submission, but it can also be a relinquishing of responsibility. We don't want to struggle with our minds, we don't want to battle with our wills. So we hand them back to God who gave them to us. The trouble is, he doesn't want them back. He wants the 'talents' he has given us to be used and to grow.

> Does your Christian learning need some 'dew from heaven' to keep it moist? Or does it need drying out a bit, to firm it up?

The problem with studying theology at University is not the critical look that is taken at the Bible and the Christian faith. It is the failure to see that, for committed Christians, this questioning is part of a personal pilgrimage for which they will need support and help. A Christian learning course takes that need seriously. It looks both at theology and at spirituality.

Christians who are exploring the meaning of their faith will always have the tension between faith and reason, between the academic and the spiritual. But it is a tension within which faith can grow strong. The struggles of the mind and the struggles of the will are both part of Christian maturity.

We 'grow up' as human beings from infancy, through adolescence, to adulthood. Our attitudes and feelings during these three stages are very different. The focus of our concern as infants is to receive love and be secure in the certainty of it. As adolescents we question everything and kick the boundaries to see how solid they are. We experiment with relationships to discover who we really are. As we become adults we continue to need love and security, we continue to question and experiment, but the focus of our lives becomes our development as people in long-term relationship with others. The development of our faith can be seen in the same kind of way.

Stages of faith

Adulthood
(the relationship)

Having shaken our foundations we now discover what (to our minds anyway) is solid and what was inadequate. We are now ready to build on a foundation which we know to be strong. We are ready for our own relationship with God, with a basic trust which is not blind to the realities of life.

Adolescence
(the questions)

Suddenly the simplicity of 'infancy faith' seems inadequate for the complex world around us. People suffer. The Church is sometimes clearly wrong. All issues look grey. This questioning is also very important, and without it our future Christian lives will be shallow.

Infancy
(the church)

Here we rest in simple trust in the truth of the gospel. God loves us. The Church's teaching is right. Issues are simple, black and white. This basic foundation of trust is very important. It may be naive, but its basic perspectives are true. Without such a foundation our future Christian lives will be unstable.

The centre of Christian faith must always be the mystical relationship with God which has always characterised the lives of the saints.

As we progress to Christian adulthood we need not leave the security of the Church behind. Nor can we omit the process of questioning, because otherwise our relationship with God will always be immature. But the centre of our attention is now our developing relationship with God, and it is around this that the certainties and the questions must revolve.

Getting stuck

But our development can get arrested. We can get stuck at one of the earlier stages.

Stuck in the Church

Those who are essentially committed to formal and traditional religion have not progressed beyond spiritual infancy. Such a life can appear humble and self-giving, but at root it is an unwillingness to grow up.

Stuck in theology

Those whose centre of attention is the intellectual questioning of Christian issues have not progressed beyond adolescence. Typically such a person is suspicious of feelings and emotion in religion, and finds it difficult to enter the more mystical aspects of faith. Often they come to believe nothing, or become rigidly orthodox in the answers that must be given to questions of faith.

Faith and culture

There is no such thing as culture-free Christianity or a culture-free gospel. Christian truth is not a pure product, found undiluted in the pages of Holy Scripture and diluted into other cultural backgrounds over the centuries.

As children, we tend to assume that the way things happen in our family is just 'normal'. In my family, Dad went out to work. Mum was always there at home. We had a holiday each summer. We had a car. We said grace at meals, without exception. That was my 'normality' as I grew up. I was aware some people did things a little differently, but that was out of the ordinary.

The beginnings of our faith within the church are also like this. Our tradition is the norm. Christian faith as it is expressed in our culture is normal. We accept that people in other countries express their Christian faith in rather different ways. But in practice we warm to those whose faith is given similar kind of expression to ours, even if the outward forms are unfamiliar to us.

When we begin a serious study of the Christian faith, what we find can be deeply disturbing.

• The culture of the Old and New Testaments turns out to be very different from ours, and perhaps we find that it is hard to identify with their concerns.

• Maybe the early Fathers and their controversies over the 'nature' of Christ and his incarnation leave us cold because they seem so barren and pointless to our modern minds.

• Perhaps we are deeply commited to the Anglican 1662 Prayer Book, but become aware that if a time machine transported us back into the 17th century, we would actually feel very out of place.

And if what we are studying is meant to be 'normal' for Christianity, where does that leave us? Culture can appear to separate us from the essentials of our faith. The truths of Christianity seem to lie rooted in cultures which are foreign to us.

Try reading the Parable of the Pounds (Luke 19:11-27) from the point of view of Christians in base communities in Nicaragua. For us the king in the story is a good character, someone who like God rightly expects the allegiance of his subjects. For them the king is a bad character, oppressing his people with the help of foreign governments; and yet opposing him leads to further oppression. This is arguably closer to the meaning the parable might have had in Jesus' day. What then might this parable mean? What is its message?

Truth is incarnate

Culture is like a language. A 'message' does not exist except within a particular language. It can be translated, but never exactly. Even the original language had its limitations in expressing the truth the person had in mind. We have to see beyond the language to the meaning. Language is just the medium through which truth is expressed.

So with culture. God's truth was expressed in particular cultures. The Hebrew world in which much of Scripture is set is a language, a medium. The truth cannot be extracted or distilled and then stored in pure form ready for reincarnation elsewhere - but it can be translated, transformed into another expression in another culture.

Some cultural expressions will be better than others. Some may distort the underlying truth and need to be challenged. But no one culture constitutes the 'normality' of Christian truth.

If we are to study Christian truth, we need an appreciation of the relation between Christianity and culture. Confusing the two is fatal for our attempt at a better understanding of Christian faith.

Doctrine develops

It is reassuring to have Creeds. We are reminded that the doctrines of the Church have been carefully worked out for us, carefully worded to protect us from error. Sometimes they are embedded into the life and worship of the church so that we take them in almost without thinking about them. Centuries later they are as true as they ever were. These and the other doctrines of the Church seem to stand as immovable pillars, stopping the church being blown about by the winds of heresy.

And yet there is another perspective. Doctrines set in stone tend to fossilise those who hold to them. Scripture itself shows us a process in which beliefs about God develop and grow. Openness to the Spirit to show us new things is integral to the appeal of the New Testament to the Jewish world to embrace Jesus as the Messiah. An appreciation of the full rights of slaves, women and children is simply not present in the Biblical record, and needed to wait for another generation, another culture.

Old teachings need to be seen afresh in each generation and culture, relating the underlying truths of them to a new and different world.

A cross-cultural experience

Alongside your studies, why not try to get to know some Christians from a totally different background from yourself? The more different they are, the better. They might come from a very different denomination or 'spirituality' background from yourself. Of they may be from a different cultural or ethnic background. Find out more about them, what they believe and how they express it.

Perspectives you gain from this will help you make the cultural adjustment in appreciating the world in which Christianity was born and interpreting it faithfully for today.

For a detailed and accessible workbook on cross-cultural Christian mission, with many practical insights about Christianity and culture, see Entering Another's World by Margaret Wardell and Robin Thomson (St John's Extension Studies 2001)

Is someone calling?

As we study the history of God's wonderful saving grace to us, and reflect on the characters who played key roles in the outworking of God's purposes, it often happens that we seem to hear God calling us. We too are committed to this saving history. We too may be used by God. We too are ordinary people like they were. Are we too being called?

Calling or 'vocation' is a contentious subject in some parts of the church. Divisions still exist over the nature of ordination and whether this is just one calling or the calling of God. We cannot resolve this specific issue here, but it is important to be clear about the nature of Christian calling.

Calling is to someone

People in full-time Christian work often talk about being called to somewhere (to another country, to a particular parish) or to something (a teaching ministry, a pastoral role). It is not hard to see why. It is clear and tangible. Sadly it sets them apart from other people.

> Mark 1:20, 2:17, 3:13, Acts 2:39, Rom. 1:6, 2 Thess. 2:13-14.

In Scripture God calls people. He speaks, and seeks a response of personal relationship with those he calls. Through the gospel message He calls people to himself. Jesus calls disciples, and they just follow him about. He seldom asked them to do anything.

If we think we hear God calling us through our studies, we need to respond to the call to belong to Him first.

Calling is to lifestyle

Christians are called to be holy. They are called to live a different kind of life from those around them, different in ways that

> Psalm 66:18, Rom. 1:7, I Cor. 1:2,9, Eph. 4:1, 1 Thess. 4:7, 1 Pet. 1:15

proclaim the essential message of the gospel. We are not called to be odd, to wear funny clothes and to be conspicuous.

Christians are also called to live out a corporate life within the Body of Christ. They are not to be solo flyers. Ironically, many who enter formal ministries in the church live a lonely existence, seeking to work out an individual ministry rather than a corporate one.

If we think we hear God calling us through our studies, we need to be working on what it means to live a holy life in our society and on how to live and work for Christ corporately with others.

Most of the text on these pages is based on material by Steve Walton, author of the book
A Call to Live (Triangle, 1994).

Calling accomplishes things

Rom. 4:17,
Rom. 8:30,
1 John 3:1

God calls us his children – and as a consequence we are! He calls Abraham to be the father of many nations – and makes sure of it! He calls sinners – and justifies them – and will bring them to glory.

God does not advertise and appoint people to 'positions' in the Kingdom on the basis of their ability, understanding and skills. He equips those who respond to His call, so that they become part of His saving purposes in the world.

If we think we hear God calling us through our studies, we can trust Him that where He sends He also equips. We can relax about apparent failure or success, because our abilities are not the basis of His calling.

Calling can be to

particular tasks or roles

With Paul's conversion came the call to be an apostle. He and Barnabas were called through the church to a wider ministry. This was 13 or 14 years after his conversion. Paul was later called specifically to take the gospel to Europe, through the dream about the man from Macedonia. That is the sum total of the NT evidence of 'calling' to particular tasks and roles.

Acts 13:1-3,
Acts 16:6-10,
Acts 26:16-18,
Rom. 1:1, 1
Cor. 1:1

The NT never identifies calling with work or jobs. God gives gifts to be exercised in the church, He does not 'call' people to exercise them. Generally He calls people to follow Him.

If we think we hear God calling us through our studies, we need to seek the help of others in the church to discover how that calling might work out in terms of tasks and roles.

MORE?

For a comprehensive workbook on Christian calling, see Fit for the Purpose by Ian Aveyard and David Muir (St John's Extension Studies, new edition due 2006). St John's also holds regular vocation weekends.

Lay?..........

The Opening up of theological education has been part of a wider movement to share the ministry and mission of the church more fully with lay men and women in local churches. 'The Ministry' had become a one-man-band, but it would now be shared with a wide group of lay people, each with their different gifts. Ministry - and ministers - had been too narrowly defined, and the stage was set for the ministry to be given back to the whole people (Greek *laos*) where it properly belonged. Extension education has been part of that movement, a resource to enable the laity to participate in the church's ministry and mission with competence and self-confidence.

....or ordained?

Today the ball-game has changed somewhat. There has been significant progress in making the clergy side of the laity/clergy divide more diverse. In the Anglican church, the advent of Non-Stipendiary Ministers (some working in industry) and the ordination of women have softened the image of an elite, class-bound, male-oriented ministry. All this is to be welcomed.

But a divide still yawns deep and wide – between the recognised and the unrecognised, between the officially trained and the not-officially trained, between the useful-in-the-church and the only-useful-in-the-world. The emphasis on a more diverse ministry has masked the greater truth that the ministry and mission of Christ belong to the whole church.

If you have no aspirations to cross the divide into recognised ministry, or have been discouraged by the church from doing so, it is important to remember that as Christ sees the church there is no such divide. The church is the body of Christ, of which he is the head. And he looks on every function within it as vitally important. By virtue of your baptism into Christ, you are part of the ministry and mission of the church. You are caught up in the work of the Kingdom of God.

Living your theology

Finally, take a moment to consider what it will mean to *live* your theology. Here are three statements to think about.

Christian theology is people-friendly

I lived for several years in India. In Eastern thought the ultimate divine reality is impersonal, beyond the restrictions of personality. The goal of salvation is to lose oneself into that divine reality, to cease to be a 'mere' person.

In Christianity God is personal, and this must be reflected in the character of our theology. It is an important criterion of Christian theology that it builds people up, not breaks them down or diminishes them. 'Right' Christian doctrines, held and supported in a way that is untrue to the character of Christian theology to be people-friendly, become demonic.

As you develop your theology, it needs to be liveable. It needs to be true as it is lived out, not just as it is formulated. In particular, you need to be able to live out the theology you develop.

Christian theology relates to current realities

God cares about our world. When Christians give answers to questions no-one is asking, they show that they do not share that concern. Our theology needs to be expressed in terms which relate to our modern world, not just to the religious concerns of the church. That is part of its validity. That is part of being true to the character of God.

Once philosophy was the necessary accompaniment to the study of theology. Society was asking 'What is true?' Today, in a society which is falling apart and does not know how to put itself together again, people are asking 'What works?' Sociology has become theology's most natural partner. This will affect how we formulate our theology and how we seek to live it out through the church.

Christian theology is part of personal development

Martin Luther rediscovered justification by faith, partly because he desperately needed to for himself. Paul was a zealous follower of God, a keen critic of new and heretical religious movements – until he 'bumped into' Jesus and discovered that he had got it all terribly wrong. It took him years to recover.

Detached intellectual enquiry into Christian theology often leads to cynicism and the loss of the vitality of faith. Christian theology is about the journey of faith – and the fierceness of the early church's theological debates reflects this. Your theology will grow as you do.

For a useful workbook on how to reflect on your Christian life and how to live out your theology, see *God Thoughts* by Ian Aveyard (St John's Extension Studies, 1997)

GLOSSARY OF COMMON THEOLOGICAL TERMS

Absolution
The declaration of the forgiveness of sins. In the R.C. tradition it is an essential part of the sacrament of reconciliation (penance).

Adoptionism
A Christological belief emphasising the complete humanity of Jesus. The term often denotes the belief that Jesus was essentially human and was elevated to divine sonship at some point in his life.

Agape
A Greek word used in the N.T. to signify God's love for humanity and the love which should bind people, especially Christians, together.

Agnosticism
Technically the belief that it is impossible to know anything which is not capable of scientific description or verification. Often used to describe an openness of mind about whether God exists or not.

Allegorical
A type of interpretation of a text which minimises the plain meaning in favour of an alleged hidden spiritual meaning.

Altruism
A selfless concern for the well being of others.

Anabaptist
Literally one who "rebaptises". Also a radical group during the Reformation period.

Analogy
The comparing of like with like. We often express our understanding of God in analogous terms. For example, "God is like a rock".

Anathema
A Greek word referring to the exclusion of heretics from the Church.

Animism
The belief that all natural phenomena are possessed by souls or spirits which animate them.

Anthropology
The study of humankind, especially in social groupings. Biblical anthropology refers to Christian doctrines about the status of humankind before God.

Anthropomorphism
The attribution of human characteristics to the activities or emotions of God.

Antinomianism
The belief that having been saved by faith, a person is free from all moral obligations.

Apocalypse
Literally "revelation". The term either refers to the N.T. book, or the end times of which it speaks.

Apocalyptic
A type of writing which uses images and symbols, usually referring to the end times.

Apocrypha
A series of books whose qualifications to be included in the canon of scripture is disputed.

Apollinarianism
A set of Christological beliefs which stressed that the centre of the human personality of Jesus was replaced by the divine Logos. The beliefs were first formulated by Apollinarius (fl. c.350 A.D.).

Apologetics
The study of how to justify Christianity in the face of other ideas or worldviews that oppose it.

Apostasy
The abandonment of Christianity for unbelief or another belief.

Arianism
The Christological theories of Arius (c.250 -336) which were condemned at the first Council of Nicaea in 323 A.D. More generally, it refers to any Christological view that makes the Logos (The Word, John 1) subordinate to God the Father.

Arminianism
The belief that people are free to choose for or against faith in Christ and that Christians can fall away from faith. It is based on the sixteenth century writings of Jacobus Arminius. It is in opposition to the views expressed in Calvinism.

Asceticism
Self-denial and self-discipline, often to an excessive degree. Sometimes used by Christians to avoid being mastered by sin. Often associated with monasticism.

Atheism
The belief that there is no God. This is not very common, since many people without faith are in fact agnostics.

Atonement.
Literally "at-one-ment". The bringing of people back into relationship with God by the forgiveness of their sin. In the O.T. atonement was brought about through animal sacrifices. In the N.T. the death of Christ is the full and final atonement.

Calvinism
A set of beliefs based on the writings of John Calvin (*Institutes of the Christian Religion*). It stresses God's sovereignty and the importance of God's predestination in a person's salvation. Calvinism is opposed to Arminianism.

Canon
The list of books belonging within the Bible. This list was finalised by the church in the fourth century.

Casuistry
The application of general moral principles to concrete ethical decisions or situations.

Catholic
A term derived from the Greek word meaning "universal" and used as a description of the whole church worldwide. It is also used to refer to the Roman Catholic Church, one of the three great traditions within Christianity.

Christology
The study of the nature and person of Jesus Christ and in particular the relation between the divine and human in him.

Consubstantial
Literally "to be of the same substance" (Gk *Homoousion*). The term was used at the Council of Nicaea to describe the relationship between the eternal Son and the Father.

Consubstantiation
The doctrine that Christ is bodily present "in, with, and under" the elements of the eucharist, although they are not essentially altered. It is based on Luther's (1483 -1546 A.D.) teaching about the eucharist and is in contrast to the doctrine of transubstantiation.

Cosmology
The study of the structure, origin and development of the universe.

Counter-Reformation
A movement for the reform of the Roman Catholic Church in the sixteenth and seventeenth centuries, partly in response to the Reformation.

Criticism (Biblical)
The scholarly study of the Bible, especially its historical background and its linguistic and literary style.

Decalogue
A name given to the ten commandments

Deism
The belief that God exists but which denies that God reveals himself or intervenes in this world in any way. This seventeenth century philosophy was the basis for the Enlightenment.

Demythologisation
The method of interpreting the N.T. as first proposed by Rudolf Bultmann in 1941. It assumes that the Gospels are prescientific and therefore mythological and that in order to gain access to the truth, scholars must "cut away" the mythological element of the narratives.

Deontological
A way of making ethical decisions based on a person's moral obligation and duties rather than on an examination of the consequences of the proposed behaviour.

Depravity (Total)
The position of humankind under the power of Original Sin. There is nothing which has not been infected by its power.

Determinism
The doctrine that human action is not free and is to be understood as the necessary outcome of certain causes.

Dialectic
The holding together of apparent contradictions and tensions in a philosophical discussion.

Dualism
The belief that there are two ultimate and self-existent realities, one good and the other evil. This is seen as an answer to the problem of evil, which God is then not responsible for.

Ekklesia
A Greek word used in the N.T. to describe the Church.

Election
The doctrine that God chooses some and not others to be the agents of his will. It is based on the Greek word meaning 'choice'.

Empiricism
A philosophical term for the view that all knowledge is ultimately derived from and tested by experience.

Enlightenment
An eighteenth century movement believing that humankind should be guided by reason and not by external authority, dogma or revelation. The movement has had a great influence on modern thought and in particular on the high place occupied by the scientific method in our pursuit of truth.

Epistemology
The philosophy of how we attain knowledge, particularly inquiring into how we know and what the sources of our knowledge are.

Eschatology
Literally "discourse about the last things". The study of the end of the age and the final end of humankind.

Essenes
A strict Jewish sect based at Qumran on the Dead Sea just before and during the time of Jesus.

Eucharist
Literally from the Greek "to give thanks" and refers to the sacrament of Holy Communion, the Mass, or Lord's Supper.

Evangelical
One who believes in the absolute authority of Scripture and that what it says is binding on all Christian people.

Evangelism
The act of sharing the good news of the gospel with others.

Ex opere operato
A Latin term to describe the view that grace is conferred through the sacraments if only minimal requisite conditions are present.

Exegesis
The process of expounding the original meaning of a text.

Existentialism
A philosophical movement which reached its zenith in the late 1940s and 50 s. It rejected externally imposed values and moral codes in favour of individuals making their own choices in terms which made sense of their own existence.

Expiation
The act of making right for an offence or injury done to some person. The term is often used with reference to the work of Christ, although some feel this does not do justice to the sacrificial imagery of the Bible. See "propitiation".

Fatalism
The belief that human destiny is shaped by impersonal spiritual forces. It often leads to an attitude of resignation.

Fathers (Early)
Key writers and thinkers in the first few Christian centuries. They played an important part in the formulation of Christian doctrine.

Flesh
Our lives and personalities when they are directed away from God. The Apostle Paul sees "the flesh" as being in total opposition to the spirit. In this context "flesh" must not be confused with the body.

Form criticism (Formgeschichte)
A method of analysing and interpreting oral traditions behind the actual texts of the Bible. Form critics believe that the writers of the Gospels collected and arranged preexisting stories about Jesus and that this material can be classified into a number of forms arising from a variety of situations.

Fundamentalism
The belief in the infallibility and inerrancy of Scripture. It is often linked to a very literalistic approach to Biblical interpretation.

Glossolalia
Literally "speaking in tongues". St Paul writes about this in 1 Cor. 12-14.

Gnosticism
A varied set of religious beliefs common in the Graeco-Roman world in N.T. times. A central belief was that salvation was attained through a secret knowledge. It saw Jesus as one mediator among many between God and humanity.

Hades
The place of departed spirits. A Greek term equivalent to the Hebrew "Sheol". Although sometimes translated "hell", it is not a place of punishment.

Heilsgeschichte
A German term meaning "salvation history". The saving acts of God to which the O.T. and N.T. bear witness.

Hellenism
The predominantly Greek culture which began with Alexander the Great and continued alongside Roman culture. It was an influential aspect of the cultural background of the N.T.

Henotheism
The worship of a single God without expressly denying the existence of other supernatural beings or deities.

Heresy
A set of beliefs considered by the church to be contrary to Christian tradition. Contrasts with "orthodoxy".

Hermeneutics
The study of how to interpret the Bible in such a way that it is both true to the original meaning of the text and relevant to contemporary culture.

Homiletics
The study of the art of preaching.

Homoousion
A Greek word, literally "of one and the same nature". The term was used in the Nicene Creed (325 A.D.) to describe the relation of the Son to the Father in the Godhead.

Humanism
A belief in the capacity of human nature to redeem itself by the aesthetic and moral senses and by education. Also a movement stressing the importance of human knowledge and learning, arising from the Renaissance.

Hypostasis
A Greek term used in the early church debate on the doctrine of the Trinity. Eventually it came to mean "individual person" and was used in the phrase "three persons in one substance".

Immanence
A term used to describe the nearness ("contactability") of God. It is usually contrasted with the Transcendence of God.

Impassible
A term often attributed to God to indicate that he is not influenced by feelings in the way human beings are.

Incarnation
Literally "taking flesh". The action of God in becoming wholly human in Jesus. In his full humanity can be seen everything about the character of God which can be conveyed in human terms.

Justification
God's act of reckoning people to be reconciled to him, despite their past sins.

Kenosis
Derived from a Greek word meaning "to empty". It was used in the N.T. and in the earliest Christological formulations to refer to the second person of the Trinity laying aside/emptying himself of all his divine attributes and assuming the limitations of human existence.

Kerygma
Derived from the Greek word for "proclaim". It normally denotes the content of the Christian proclamation - what God has done for men and women in the life, death and resurrection of Jesus.

Laity
Derived from a Greek word meaning "people". It is usually used to distinguish the non-ordained Christian from one who is ordained.

Legalism
The approach to religion which sees the keeping of laws and regulations as central.

Liberal
A type of theology which asserts its freedom to question accepted authorities. It is often critical of orthodox Christianity.

Liberation Theology
A movement which has spread from Latin America since the early 1960s. It is concerned with the application of Christian belief to situations of oppression and political injustice.

Liturgy
A set form of worship, usually published in a book. Liturgy is usually followed word by word but sometimes simply provides a framework for worship.

Logos
A Greek word normally translated "Word". In the early church it was used to express the mind or reason of God which was perfectly seen and embodied in the person of Jesus.

Marcionite
Following the teachings of Marcion who was excommunicated in Rome in c.144 A.D. He rejected the Old Testament and made a strong distinction between the loving Father of Jesus and the God of the Old Testament.

Materialism
The theory that all reality is essentially matter and that all human activity can be explained without reference to the mind or spirit. It can also mean a tendency to prefer material possessions and physical comfort to spiritual values.

Mediaeval
Pertaining to the time of the Middle Ages. In Christian thought this period was characterised by the attempt to harmonise Biblical teaching with the philosophy of Aristotle.

Metaphysical
Those things which are beyond the realms of physical observation. The term can also be used of the study of what is fundamental to Being.

Millennium
A thousand year period. It is often associated with the period prophesied in the book of Revelation when the righteous will rule the earth.

Millennialism
The belief that there will be a thousand year period when the kingdom of God will flourish. Millennialists tend to fall into two camps : 1) those who believe that the second coming of Christ will come *before* the millennium (premillennialism) and 2) those who believe that Christ will come again only *after* the millenium (postmillennialism).

Modalism
A doctrine of God which denies the distinct personhood of Father, Son and Holy Spirit. Each person is seen as merely a different aspect (or "mode") of God's existence.

Monism
The belief that all things, material and immaterial, personal and impersonal, are essentially one fundamental reality. It is the underlying belief of Hinduism.

Monophysitism
A Christological belief which held that Jesus had only one nature in him after the incarnation and that it was divine. This view was common in the fourth century after the Council of Chalcedon and was in contradiction to the declaration of the Council that Jesus had two complete natures in one person, human and divine.

Monotheism
The belief that there is only one God. A fundamental belief of Christianity, Islam and Judaism.

Mystery
Something that we can know but never fully understand.

Mysticism
The pursuit of the interior life of the spirit through spiritual exercises and discipline in the attempt to know and experience the divine at the deepest possible level. There is a long tradition of mysticism within Christianity and within other religions.

Myth
A powerful story which expresses or encapsulates truths (religious or other). It may also teach a moral code or explain ritual. Some Christians would see the early chapters of Genesis as mythological.

Natural law
The theory that there are inherent universal structures of human existence which may be discerned by human reason and which form the basis for judgments of conscience. The theory of Natural Law underpins the thought of Thomas Aquinas and much Roman Catholic ethical teaching.

Natural revelation
The revelation of God as seen in creation. This is distinct from the special revelation of God as seen in the Old and New Testaments.

Natural theology
The attempt to build a doctrine of God on the basis of reason and experience alone. There is no appeal made to faith or special revelation.

Neo-orthodoxy

A type of twentieth century theology which reacted to earlier Liberal theology and emphasises the importance of the revelation of God through the Word of God. The term is often used to describe the writings of Karl Barth.

Nestorianism

A term referring to the Christological beliefs of Nestorius, who became Bishop of Constantinople in A.D. 428. Scholars are uncertain of his exact beliefs. The term is normally used to describe the belief that the divine and human in Christ were not fully united.

Nominalism

A theory of knowledge particularly associated with William of Occam (c.1300 - c.1349). He held that universal concepts had no separate or independent reality but were simply names used to organise things with similar characteristics. The theory was in contrast with "realism" which held that a universal concept was more real than the individual manifestation of it - e.g. the concept of "humanity" is more real than any individual person.

Numinous

An inner sense of spiritual realities beyond our everyday material lives.

Omnipotence

Being all powerful, the possession of the perfect form of power. A term usually applied to God alone.

Omnipresence

The attribute applied to God to indicate his presence everywhere.

Omniscience

Literally "the knowing of all things". An attribute usually applied to God alone.

Ontological Argument

The name given to one of the "proofs" of the existence of God. The thesis is that in the very nature of things, logic demands that a being must exist who is greater than everything else.

Original sin

The predisposition towards sin which is part of fallen human nature. This predisposition is believed to have originated from the Fall (Genesis 3).

Orthodoxy

Literally "right teaching". In theology it means Christian teaching held to be true by the established church, and is in contrast to heresy.

Panentheism

The belief that everything exists in God, but that creation does not exhaust God's being as God also transcends it.

Pantheism

The belief that all things are divine. Many pantheists worship nature.

Paraclete

Literally "one who is called alongside". The name given to the Holy Spirit in John's gospel.

Parousia

A Greek term meaning "coming" and "presence". Usually refers to the second coming of Christ.

Passion (of Christ)

The suffering experienced by Jesus as his death approached. Usually refers to the time from the prayer in the Garden of Gethsemene to his death on the cross.

Patristics

The study of the life, writings and thought of the theologians of the early church.

Pelagianism

A set of beliefs based on the the teachings of Pelagius (c.400) about the relationship between divine grace and the human will. He denied the existence of original sin and emphasised the importance of the freedom of the human will. St. Augustine attacked Pelagianism as he believed it implied the possibility that humanity could save itself and had no need for grace.

Phenomenology (of religions)

A method of studying religion where the scholar does not judge the beliefs of a religion as true or false but tries to see the world as the believer sees it.

Pietistic

A term used to describe activities which put great emphasis on the need for devotion and holiness. The Pietists were a seventeenth and eighteenth century movement within Protestantism.

Platonic

Teaching based on the ideas of the Greek philosopher Plato (427-347 B.C.). He held that this world is a copy of the "ideal forms" to which human eternal souls belonged.

Pluralism

The belief that all religions and world views are equally valid, and that truth claims by one imply a disparagement of all others.

Pneumatology

In classical philosophy the term refers to the study of the nature of the human soul. In Christian theology it refers to the study of the person and work of the Holy Spirit.

Polytheism

The belief that there are many gods.

Positivism

The philosophical belief that all true knowledge consists of matters of fact or logic. This is in contrast to "speculative" philosophy, which allows value judgments to have the status of knowledge as well.

Praxis

The application of Christian belief which starts from concrete situations, particularly those of injustice and oppression. It is a fundamental element of Liberation Theology and its hermeneutics.

Predestination

God's foreordaining of a person's life and eternal destiny. This has always been difficult to reconcile with ideas of free will and the individual's own step of repentance and faith. It is associated with the teaching of John Calvin.

Prevenient grace

In Roman Catholic teaching it refers to the supernatural power which quickens and assists the will to have faith. In Protestantism it is generally used to refer to the grace preceding the individual's decision of faith but does not imply a special quickening.

Preexistence (of Christ)

Being in existence before creation. Christians believe that not only was God the Father preexistent but that the Son of God, the Logos, was also preexistent. This is in contrast to the teaching of Arius (d.336).

Process theology

A theology which emphasises process over against unchanging being and substance. God Himself is involved in processes and is thus not an unchanging God.

Propitiation

The act of appeasing the wrath of a deity by offering a suitable sacrifice. Some view the death of Christ in this way, although others are uncomfortable about seeing Christ's death as an appeasement and prefer to see it as God's self-giving. See "expiation".

Proselyte

A Gentile converted to Judaism. The term can also be used to refer to any person converted from one creed to another.

Rationalism
A seventeenth and eighteenth century philosophical movement which valued reason as the ultimate arbiter of all statements. Rationalists frequently question the existence of any special revelation from God.

Regeneration
Literally "rebirth". The term is used to refer to the renewing of the self which occurs when God's grace is accepted. In Roman Catholic teaching regeneration has traditionally been identified with the reception of the sacraments.

Reincarnation
The belief that all souls live a series of succeeding lives within animals and within human beings. An important belief in Hinduism.

Renaissance
Literally 'rebirth'. A movement in the fourteenth, fifteenth and sixteenth centuries which marks the end of the mediaeval period. During this period there was a new freedom to think out beliefs in a fresh way, rather than being bound entirely by the past.

Revelation
God's action in making himself known to the world.

Sacrament
St. Augustine described this as "an outward and visible sign of an inward and spiritual grace". It is a rite in which God's saving grace is active. Baptism and the Eucharist are sacraments but Roman Catholics would also add confirmation, marriage, ordination, reconciliation, and extreme unction.

Sanctification
Literally "being made holy". The process by which the believer's life and character are changed into the likeness of Christ, through the work of the Holy Spirit.

Schism
A division of the Church. The most important of these have been the schism between Western and Eastern Christianity in the eleventh century, and the Reformation in the sixteenth century.

Scholasticism
A type of thinking which accepts a certain teacher as authoritative and then refines and extends the teaching given. The term is particularly applied to mediaeval scholars who devoted themselves to the teaching of Aristotle. Their approach often used logic, debate and speculation.

Secularism
A world view which takes no account of traditional world faiths and often denies the existence of the spiritual dimension. It is characteristic of the modern western world.

Septuagint
The Greek translation of the O.T. including the Apocrypha. It is said to have been made about 270 B.C. by seventy translators. It is often abbreviated as the Roman numeral for 70, LXX.

Sheol
The name given in the O.T. to the place where the spirits of the dead reside. See "Hades".

Situation Ethics
An approach to making ethical decisions which gives primary importance to the situation/context of the decision rather than to moral codes or principles. The highest intrinsic good is love and love must always be served in the situation.

Social gospel
An influential American movement in the late nineteenth and early twentieth century which emphasised collective sin and social salvation. The kingdom of God was seen as a work of God focussed entirely on the transformation of this present world. It was closely identified with liberal Protestantism.

Soteriology
The study of the doctrine of salvation.

Stoicism
A Greek philosophical movement founded by Zeno (c.300 B.C.). It saw the universe as permeated by Mind or Reason, and human beings as needing to live according to reason. It was ascetic in nature.

Subordinationism
A view of the Trinity in which the Son is thought to be subordinate to the Father, or the Holy Spirit is thought to be subordinate to both.

Syncretism
An attempt to combine together different and apparently divergent teachings and doctrines. This may be within one faith or between faiths.

Synoptic (Gospels)
Literally "viewed in the same way". The term refers to the Gospels of Matthew, Mark and Luke, because John's portrayal of Jesus is so different.

Teleology
Often used in ethics to describe the process by which the means of an action are justified by the ends of the action. It also refers to one of the classical "proofs" of the existence of God, arising from the question of the purpose of existence.

Theism
The belief in one unified being which, although distinct from the cosmos, is the source of it and continues to sustain it. Theism is usually contrasted with Pantheism.

Theodicy
The attempt to justify the goodness of an omnipotent God in the face of the evil and suffering seen in the world.

Theophany
A manifestation of God in some tangible form. The transfiguration is an example.

Tractarianism
A nineteenth century Anglican movement which attempted to reinstate the Church's Catholic heritage.

Transcendent
Something which extends beyond human and earthly concerns. An attribute often associated with God, and contrasted with "immanence".

Transubstantiation
The Roman Catholic belief that the substance of the elements of bread and wine are transformed by priestly consecration into the substance of the body and blood of Jesus Christ.

Tritheism
An extreme Trinitarian belief in three separate and distinct persons sharing the nature of deity. It denies the orthodox belief in the essential unity of the Trinity.

Unitarianism
The belief that only God the Father is divine and that the Son and the Spirit are not God.

Universalism
The belief that everyone will eventually receive salvation, even if they have no faith in Christ.

Vulgate
An influential Latin translation of the Bible undertaken in the 4th century A.D. This became the standard Bible of the mediaeval church.

Zealots
A Jewish sect in the first century A.D. which tried to overthrow the Roman occupying army by force.

Faith for Life

is a series of A4 workbooks designed to help you think through important issues from a Christian point of view. Each book looks at a topic of concern to Christian people and helps them towards a clearer understanding of the Christian faith. The books can be used

- as a resource for your own life
- as the basis of group study
- as a way of earning credits towards the St John's *Certificate in Christian Studies*.

Current titles:

The World Christian (Robin Thomson): What does it mean to be a member of the world church, where Christians from many cultures struggle together to learn about mission in a 'pluralistic' world?

Entering Another's World (Margaret Wardell & Robin Thomson): A more practical expolration of how cultures differ. A real preparation for moving from one culture to another.

Fit for the Purpose (David Muir): If you are trying to understand what God wants for your life, this book will help you discern that 'vocation' and respond appropriately.

God Thoughts (Ian Aveyard): The term 'theological reflection' is a bit off-putting, though every Christin does threology whether they realise it or not.

Leading Children (Penny Frank & Nick Harding): Designed to encourage reflection in those who lead children in a Christian context. Especially helpful for those who 'lead the leaders'.

Something in Common (Adrian Chatfield): An introduction to the practice and principles of worldwide Anglicanism. What does it mean to belong to this diverse body of Christians?

Sustaining the Earth (Tim Cooper): Why does Christianity have such a bad press when it comes to concern for the environment? A challenge to rethink your apathy about our struggling planet.

The Vital Connection (John Goldingay): A challenge to deepen your own spirituality by examining what has been helpful in your Christian life so far and introducing you to new resources.

In Search of Wholeness (Russ Parker, Derek Fraser and David Rivers): A journey through the Church's ministry of healing for the benefit of both volunteers and health professionals.

Coming soon:

Different Expressions of Christianity (Elizabeth Fisher): An exploration of the worldwide ecumenical movement including the current challenges that face the Christian churches.

For more details, or to order your copy, either telephone St John's on 0115 925 1117 or visit www.stjohns-nottm.ac.uk

ST JOHN'S
NOTTINGHAM